ISLAND PILOT

ISLAND PILOT

by

Captain Alan Whitfield

The Shetland Times Ltd.,
Lerwick.
1995

Copyright © Alan Whitfield 1995.
First published by The Shetland Times Ltd., 1995.

Cover design by the Stafford Partnership, Shetland.

Cover photographs: Front: Captain Alan Whitfield © Scotsman Publications,
Edinburgh. First Loganair ambulance flight at Tingwall © Dennis Coutts.
Back: Foula airstrip.

ISBN 1 898852 05 7

British Library Cataloguing-in-Publication Data
A catalogue record for this book is available from the British Library.

Printed and published by The Shetland Times Ltd.,
Prince Alfred Street, Lerwick, Shetland ZE1 0EP.

List of illustrations

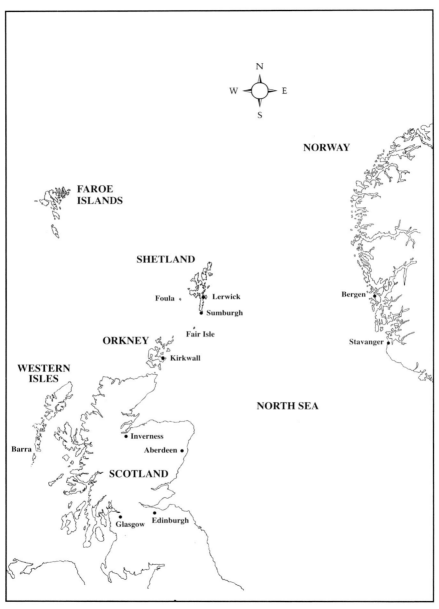

Geographical position of Britain's northerly islands.

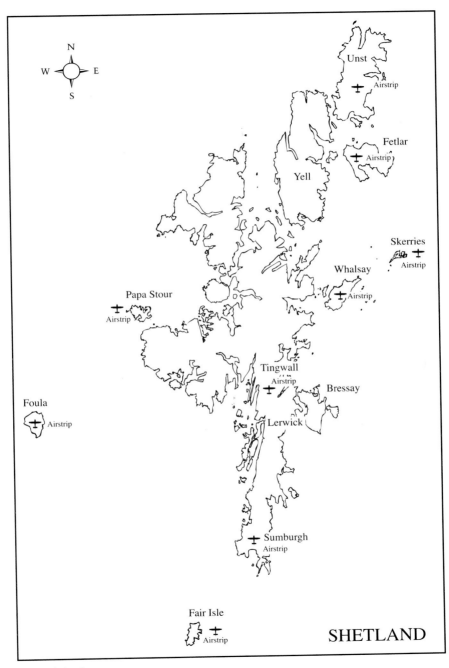

Shetland airstrips.

Preface

Shetland consists of about 100 islands lying on and to the north of the sixtieth degree of latitude. This is about the same distance north as the southern tip of Greenland and Hudson's Bay in Canada. About 15 of these islands are inhabited and today are linked by a very efficient ferry system that was made possible by the revenue brought to the islands by North Sea oil. The oil boom in the 1970s also brought enormous improvements to the airports of Sumburgh, Sullom Voe and Unst, enabling airlines to improve their services to Shetland to a level once believed to be impossible with the finances then available.

In 1969 internal transport within the islands was by an interlinked bus and ferry system operated with boats that were basically converted fishing boats. These only operated on a limited basis and not every day in winter. They were unable to carry any vehicles or heavy goods and were very vulnerable to adverse weather. A larger steamer, the *Earl of Zetland*, provided heavy transport capabilities but was unable to berth at some of the smaller islands where disembarking was by "flit boat" which was even more dependent on weather.

Air services were provided by British European Airways, the forerunner of today's British Airways. They flew a service six days a week via Orkney with an extra service on some days direct from Aberdeen. The aircraft used was the Viscount, an excellent machine, but not suited to the limited facilities provided at Sumburgh leading to many cancellations when the weather was bad. BEA also provided an ambulance service with Heron aircraft to the mainland of Scotland. Within Shetland patients were evacuated by ferry, fishing boat, or the lifeboats, a very lengthy process.

Navigation facilities for aircraft were very limited consisting in the main of an old-fashioned radio beacon at Sumburgh and a very low-powered VOR beacon with a marker beacon, somewhat derogatorily called the "Scotsman's instrument landing system" by pilots. This offered a very limited instrument approach capability. There was one air traffic controller who also acted as airport manager and weather observer. He only manned the control tower for the arrival of BEA services and ambulance flights.

This was the situation when I went to Shetland in 1969 and which Loganair hoped to change.

Introduction

The ringing telephone dragged me from sleep and as I walked to the front hall to answer it I was aware of an unexplained sense of unease.

"Hello Alan, Ian here. There is a problem in Fair Isle. Can we get over there as soon as possible?"

As I reached for the air ambulance pad to record the details I realised the cause of my unease - the Sumburgh fog horn was blowing! Looking out of the window I could see right across the airfield but the base of the cloud was very low; the lighthouse at Sumburgh is about 300 feet up and it was obviously in cloud.

"It's not very good Ian. How important is it that we go now?"

"Very."

"Roger, I'll call you right back."

Next I called Stewart Thomson on Fair Isle. Living in a small community he already was aware of the emergency and had checked outside.

"The North Light is blowing but not the South and I can see well to the south of the island."

This confirmed my assessment of the situation. The North Lighthouse is high up on the cliffs whilst the south one is at sea level. This suggested a cloud base of about 250 feet. The airstrip on Fair Isle is about 400 feet up - it was going to be tricky!

There was a lot more phoning to do; the doctor to tell him I would have a go, the air traffic controller to get the airfield opened up, the Aberdeen Met office to check on diversion airfields in case the weather in Shetland closed in completely and, finally, Stewart in Fair Isle to give him an ETA (estimated time of arrival) and tell him how I wanted the old-fashioned paraffin flares positioned.

In the days before the oil boom hit Shetland everyone lent a hand and by the time I reached the airfield the aircraft was refuelled, one of the firemen was helping fit the stretcher and all was ready to go.

Twenty-eight minutes later my logbook shows that the doctor and I were airborne. At 150 feet I found that the aircraft was just clear of the cloud and so set course for the island. After about five minutes fog right down to the sea forced me to climb and at 450 feet we emerged into bright moonlight with the fog a milky sea beneath. The visibility was good on top and we could see the top of Ward Hill on Fair Isle standing out clearly.

Passing over the island the gooseneck flares were just visible through the cloud so, turning left, I started an approach only to lose sight of everything as I entered the fog, forcing a climb back up into the moonlight. This clearly would not do and as I had no contact with Fair Isle I was entirely on my own. I called the controller at Sumburgh who telephoned Fair Isle and learned that it was still clear beneath the cloud to the south.

With this in mind I positioned the aircraft to the south and began a very cautious descent through the cloud layer, finally getting in sight of the sea at about 200 feet with the lighthouse clearly visible to the north. Returning towards the island I turned right to follow the shoreline, keeping it about 400 yards off my port wing. The Sheep Rock came into sight, then the Bird Observatory and as I flew past parallel to the coast I could just see the glow of the goosenecks at the end of the strip. Slowing the aircraft down I put down some flap and, lining up with the edge of a cliff which is off the end of the strip, I started an approach. As I progressed I realised that I would enter the cloud as I climbed up the hillside towards the strip. My only chance would be if I could catch a glimpse of the first flares before I had to put on full power and climb away to a safe height.

I continued the approach watching out for a small walled enclosure, known in Shetland as a "planticrub", a place used to raise cabbage plants, which I knew was about 100 yards before the strip. I decided that if I lost sight of that before seeing the flares I would have to overshoot. I reached it and started to open the throttles at the same instant seeing the glow of the first flare. Selecting full flap I closed the throttles and slammed the aircraft onto the strip standing on the brakes as soon as it touched. As soon as we had stopped I taxied over to where the vehicles were waiting for us and as the doctor was driven off down to the patient I sat in a state of exhilarated relief at being on the ground.

By the time the doctor returned with the patient the fog had closed in totally and visibility was down to yards. I was able to talk to Sumburgh on the radio and was told that conditions there were unchanged so, taxi-ing to the west end of the strip, I made a blind take-off out over the sea. The return to Sumburgh was fairly routine and soon the patient was on her way to hospital whilst I returned home to relax with a cup of tea.

Of all the hundreds of ambulance flights I carried out during my career that is the one which sticks most in my memory and about which I still wake up sometimes in the night and shudder.

This is the story of how I came to be there.

Chapter One

I first saw Shetland as I was to see it so many times, a grey mass of rock looming up out of the mist as I crept in low over the sea to land on Runway 27 at Sumburgh. I was flying a Piper Aztec, a small twin-engined aircraft with seats for five people which was for many years the workhorse of the Highland aviation scene. In the back were some journalists rushing up to Fetlar to cover the defection of a Russian seaman; at that time there was no airstrip on Fetlar and the rest of their journey would be completed by road.

The terminal building at Sumburgh in those days was a wartime hut left over from the days when Sumburgh was a front line airfield; in one end of it Jim Black (the only BEA superintendent to breed his own staff) ruled the roost, whilst at the other a small cafeteria provided soup and rolls. As the day was dank and with very poor visibility I retired into this building to drink tea and await the indefinite return of my passengers. After about an hour a lightening appeared in the sky and suddenly, as often happens in Shetland, the sun burst through, the mist disappeared and the rocky splendours of Fitful Head and the rest of the Ness appeared. As there was no word of the return of my passengers I took a walk alongside the Pool of Virkie and on out to the Brochhead. Sitting for a while on the grass watching the sea and the birds I decided that I had to come and live here.

At that time I was working for a charter company based near Perth and how I would ever manage to find a job in Shetland was not very clear but as I flew in and out of Sumburgh over the next two years the determination grew to achieve this aim. Loganair, then run by the legendary Captain Mac, started the Orkney inter-island service in conjunction with the Orkney Islands Shipping Company. The service had been in abeyance since the end of World War Two but with grants from the Scottish Office and the goodwill and active assistance of the Orkney County Council it was soon up and running. I often chatted to Jim Lee, the resident pilot, on frequent trips to Orkney and one day over a cup of coffee, at some airport where we had happened to meet, I told Captain Mac that if ever he decided to start a similar service in Shetland I would be glad to go and run it for him.

Nothing happened for another year but the frequency of my trips to the islands increased, particularly during one of the transport strikes when for a while I was in and out two or three times a day. About this time the army, under the Operation Military Aid To The Community (OPMAC) scheme, built an airstrip in Unst and I added this to my ports of call.

With the addition of a strip at the north end of Shetland the way was now open for an attempt to start an internal air service and soon after this I received a call from Captain Mac to say that Loganair was going to base an aircraft in Shetland from the beginning of September 1969 and did I want the job. I immediately told the family that we were off to the north, gave my notice in to my current employer and started planning our move. The first essential was somehere to live but a telephone call to Tommy Burgess at Quendale solved this with the offer of a house to rent at Sandsayre.

Came July and we were on the move. The family went by sea on the *St Clair* whilst my son and I, with the help of a friend, launched our sailing cruiser at Fraserburgh and set sail. All went smoothly on the trip north until when about 10 miles to the south of Sumburgh Head the Sumburgh Light disappeared into a fog bank rolling in from the east. Soon we were in it too and with the aid of our DF set we found ourselves creeping through the Roost, round the Head and then cautiously into the Pool of Virkie to anchor about 9.00am after 26 hours at sea.

Our hopes of a well-earned sleep were soon shattered by a welcoming party from the airport fire brigade in their rescue craft led, I seem to remember, by Robbie Burgess who was to become a firm friend in the years to come.

Our furniture arrived later that day and we had our first experience of the Shetland helpfulness as the whole of the airport staff arrived at the same time to help us move in. Various ladies followed bearing food ready prepared and soon a roaring party, the first of many to follow over the years, was underway.

Two days later, having settled in, I was on my way to Glasgow to start learning to fly the Britten-Norman Islander. The Islander, a rugged twin-engined aircraft, built at that time in the Isle of Wight, was to be the mainstay of island flying for the foreseeable future. Capable of carrying nine passengers or nearly a ton of freight it could also be turned in a matter of minutes into a very effective air ambulance equipped with much essential medical equipment. It was once described "as an aeroplane it is a good farm tractor". Capable of using the smallest and roughest of airstrips it had appeared on the market at just the right time for the development of air services in the north and Loganair was its first commercial operator. Over the next few years I was to fly over 5,000 hours in it and it never let me down.

The first step in converting to a new type of aeroplane is to learn all about the technical details before writing an exam set by the Airworthiness Division of the CAA, or the Air Registration Board as it was known at that time. This was a bigger task than usual as the ARB had agreed that, due to the remoteness of the operation, dispensation would be given to allow me to carry out certain regular maintenance tasks on the aeroplane myself. This meant that I had to spend some time in the hangar with the engineers learning how to accomplish this. In addition to the normal written examination I also had to satisfy an ARB inspector that I was competent to perform this task.

I then had to learn how to fly the aeroplane: in particular how to deal with any possible emergency such as the failure of one engine, a particularly easy

To the left of this photograph, which was taken by Dennis Coutts in 1964, is the wartime airstrip on Fair Isle.

task this as the single-engined performance was very good. With its fixed undercarriage and simple systems the Islander is ideal for operation in remote and arduous locations and this also makes it an easy aircraft to convert to.

Finally, all formalities completed, I left Glasgow on Saturday, 12th September, 1969 on board a BEA Viscount bound for Kirkwall where I was met by Jim Lee, then the resident Loganair pilot in Orkney, who informed me that he had a flight booked to Fair Isle that evening and would take me along to teach me how to land there.

At that time Fair Isle airstrip was a wartime relic 1,200 feet long and only 22 feet wide carved out of the hillside. As the Islander wheels were about 14

3

feet apart it left little room for error especially if, as often happened, the wind was blowing across the strip. On arrival he pointed out the places where turbulence was to be expected, warned me not to attempt landing in certain wind conditions, sat beside me while I flew one or two approaches and landings and then we flew back to Kirkwall where I stayed the night. That evening in the bar I met up with the Lerwick lifeboat crew who were on the way north with their newly overhauled boat, an evening which led to a long friendship with Peter Leith, then deputy coxswain to his brother George. This, in the fullness of time, led me to being invited to join them in their squad at Up-Helly-A', a great honour indeed. But that was a year away yet.

The next morning, with Islander G-AVRA, I flew up to Sumburgh laden down with all the bits and pieces necessary to start operating. I was met by a welcoming committee consisting of my wife and family, now well settled in, and the late Captain Jack Leask, a retired BEA pilot, who some 20 years previously had been the last resident Shetland pilot when he flew a De Havilland Rapide of Scottish Airways, before going on to a career which saw him retire as a jet captain. Jack lived in a house on the hill above the airfield and, after helping us to push the Islander into the hangar, invited us home with him to share what was to be the first of many drams with him and his wife Meg over the years.

The next day I finished moving all the office gear into what had been the old wartime hospital block at the airport and then at 0950 took off on the first of many hundreds of flights to Fair Isle. Loganair's Shetland air service had started.

Chapter Two

At that time, apart from the main airport at Sumburgh, there were only three airstrips available in Shetland; Fair Isle, the new airstrip at Unst to which we hoped we would soon be operating a daily service, and the old wartime airfield at Scatsta, which was largely covered by a US Navy installation but had part of one runway which could be used for charter work.

The priorities therefore were to get a daily service operating, to find sites for strips on as many islands as possible and to find ways of getting them built. The first objective seemed straightforward. We had the air service licence already granted; the Unst airstrip was built; and all that was needed was for the Zetland County Council to provide fire cover and get the strip licensed for scheduled services. As we had reason to believe from previous meetings and correspondence that the council welcomed our efforts, we expected that this would go through very quickly.

In those days, when facilities were very limited at Sumburgh, it was not unusual for bad weather to result in the cancellation of the scheduled service provided by BEA from the south and when this happened we were often chartered by *The Daily Express* and the GPO to fly to Kirkwall, taking the outgoing mail south and bring back the daily papers and incoming mail. Any empty space we sold as seats to stranded passengers at the normal BEA rates and used this extra revenue to discount the charter rate to the newspapers, not exactly legal as the air service regulations stood at that time but the authorities turned a blind eye.

One of the most frequent passengers on these flights was Lord Jo Grimond, then the local MP, and on one of the earliest he told me that he was staying in Scalloway for the weekend and would like me to call on him on Sunday morning to talk about Loganair's plans for Shetland. When I arrived at the hotel I found that by coincidence the Foula boatman, Ken Gear, was staying there, also having been unable to return to the island due to the same bad weather which had caused the cancellation of the regular flight from Orkney on the Friday. This was an added bonus as Foula was nearly impossible to reach on a day trip during the winter and to get the chance to talk about airstrips to an inhabitant was an opportunity too good to miss.

Over the years many attempts to land on Foula had been made, all of them ending in some sort of trouble. Indeed, on the most recent some years previously, an aircraft had been stranded there for many weeks after bogging down when landing on what from the air had appeared to me to be the best area. Ken told me that the legendary Captain Fresson had intended constructing a strip there after Highland Airways had had to make an emergency food drop there in the late Thirties; a site had been found and preparatory work had been carried out but the war had stopped it.

The site was on the South Ness and a section of banking had been removed in order to get the necessary length and Ken thought that this area offered the best chance of quickly getting an emergency strip into operation. We had by now been joined by a reporter from *The Daily Express*, Bill Allsopp, who, sensing a story, agreed to go over to Foula with Ken to see what could be done. Three days later I got a phone call from him to say that they had marked out a minimal strip with whitewashed stones and that the ground appeared to be firm and smooth enough to permit a landing. That afternoon I flew over to have a look myself.

The strip, on the cliffs at the south end of the island, was very short, at 300 yards the absolute minimum that I thought I could get away with, and sloped very steeply uphill. I tried several approaches and quickly realised that it would be a one-way strip - land uphill and take off downhill regardless of wind direction. On my last approach I briefly ran my wheels along the strip and returned to Sumburgh feeling that on the first suitable day I would fly over and attempt a landing. This was on 16th October and it was not until 4th November that a suitable day, clear and with a very light breeze from the west, occurred. I rang up Lerwick photographer, Dennis Coutts, a man of strong nerves or great faith in my ability, who was to accompany me on several first landings during the next year. He agreed to come long and at 12.25 we touched down on Foula. The population of the island numbered 33 at that time and 31 of them were there to greet us, the only exceptions being a very old lady who was bedridden and someone who had stayed at home to look after her.

The strip was indeed very short but very smooth turf and, with the exception of an odd boggy patch carefully marked for me, seemed as though in reasonable weather conditions it could be used with very light loads for emergencies.

Half-an-hour later, after talking to everyone present and Dennis having recorded the event, I started up and after taxi-ing to the very top of the strip turned round and surveyed the downward slope ending on the cliff top, with some trepidation. I picked a marker far enough down the slope to show me a point from which I thought I could stop before going over the edge if anything went wrong. Opening up to full power I released the brakes and we were off. About two-thirds of the way to my marker the aircraft had reached minimum flying speed and I lifted it off the ground, holding it low over the cliffs to reach a safe speed before climbing away to come round for a low pass and return to Sumburgh. The first of the island airstrips was in being.

Just eight days later the strip was used in anger for the first time to carry out an ambulance flight to the Lerwick hospital.

In the meantime, at the invitation of the local boatman and Dennis and Stella Shepherd, the missionary and school teacher, I had been over to Papa Stour and found a possible strip on the common grazing in the centre of the island. It was very rough but I marked out an area 400 yards long and 10 yards wide which was my preferred minimum airstrip and explained to them what work would be necessary to get it fit to land on.

The next day Mr Shepherd rung me up to say that they had had a meeting and all the island men, numbering seven I think, were going to start work immediately. By early December, using only picks and shovels and a small tractor, they had the work completed and again accompanied by the intrepid Dennis Coutts I landed on Papa Stour for the first time on 10th December.

In great contrast to all this enthusiastic self-help our attempts to get the scheduled service started were completely bogged down. There was an element among the more influential members of the county council at that time who

Clearing the site for the proposed airstrip on Papa Stour, 1970. The quote on the front cover of this book was the reply Dennis Shepherd received when he asked Captain Whitfield what he required for a landing strip.
Photo: © D. H. Shepherd

appeared to be absolutely against a scheduled service. Dark mutterings of vested interests were heard in the islands and by mid-December letters were appearing in *The Shetland Times*. It was to be the beginning of a love-hate relationship with the council which was to dog all my time in Shetland.

All that was required to enable us to start was the granting of a licence for the Unst airstrip, and to achieve this the council had to provide very minimal fire cover at the strip and two men to man it. The equipment had already been

The first airstrip on Papa Stour – the markers are visible to the left of the scattald dyke.

Photo: © D. H. Shepherd

Landing on the cleared airstrip, 1970.

Photo: © D. H. Shepherd

purchased and the Board of Trade, then the responsible authority, had offered to train the two roads department employees who where to do the job, free of charge, but all sorts of excuses were being made to avoid the issue. A similar block appeared to exist within the local health board and doctors were being pressured not to call on the Islander for ambulance flights if a ferry could be used. Several ignored this pressure and indeed one doctor was told that he would be personally billed for one flight he had called for. I believe he had made very short shrift of that suggestion.

All these delaying tactics had their effect and the start of the schedule was still four months away. I was, however, very busy with charter flights with an increasing number to Unst whenever bad weather prevented the ferry service operating. I also visited Orkney regularly, Wick, Aberdeen, Glasgow, Edinburgh and Inverness, several of the flights being to carry councillors and officials to meetings as at that time there was only a once-a-day service from Scotland. By chartering a return to Shetland could be made the same day. I was also called on occasionally to carry out ambulance flights within Orkney when their aircraft was busy.

The first official landing on Papa Stour, in December 1970, accompanied by Dennis Coutts who took this commemorative photograph of the residents who turned out to welcome them.
Photo: © Dennis Coutts

9

We were always looking for any opportunity to increase the revenue of the infant operation and one day it was suggested that as fresh fruit was almost unknown in Shetland at that time (it came in on the boat from Aberdeen and took days often to arrive on the shelf) we might make a little towards the cost of positioning empty aeroplanes from Glasgow by loading up with fruit straight from the market on the day of the flight. This proved immensely popular and thereafter, until the supply of fresh goods became routine when the oil boom started, we regularly brought in about half a ton of fruit and vegetables which rapidly sold out after the aircraft's arrival.

Shetland's taste in fruit at that time was very limited and we were caught out once or twice before we realised this, and tried things like a case of grapefruit. Any flight to Aberdeen on a Sunday always collected a load of Sunday papers as they normally didn't arrive until Monday at that time. A very efficient grapevine operated in the islands and there was always a crowd of people, often Lerwick folks, awaiting our return.

In January Bobby Tulloch from Yell took me over to Fetlar to meet the people and look for a site for a strip. We quickly found an excellent site and I marked it out. Fetlar had been visited by air once pre-war on a survey by Highland Airways, a De Havilland Rapide having landed there on that occasion. However again the war had intervened and the area used was no longer suitable. The men of the island agreed that they would start work as soon as possible on a minimum sized strip.

The whole Shetland operation was a family operation; my wife, Viv, ran the office side of things, acted as ground hostess and coped with any eventuality, and on Saturdays my son and elder daughter washed and cleaned the aeroplane. In addition to our normal work we also dispensed fuel, which at that time came in in 40 gallon barrels, to the occasional itinerant aircraft which passed through. The total amount of Avgas we used was too small to interest the company which held the fuel concession for the airport, so we had to supply and serve ourselves.

I also spent a day or two in Orkney with Jim Lee to qualify on the Orkney strips so that I was available to help out in an emergency. Four days later I was called upon to do an ambulance flight from Stronsay to Inverness, the first of many I was to carry out in Orkney.

The pattern continued for the next two months, including a whole week doing the Orkney inter-island service, and in April I had my first emergency, though it was to have an amusing result.

I had been called to Papa Westray to take a sick patient to Aberdeen. The flight down was uneventful and after having a cup of coffee we were ready to return to Sumburgh. I asked the nurse who had accompanied the patient if she would like to fly back in the front seat next to me to see what went on at the sharp end of the aeroplane. She accepted with enthusiasm and we took off. The intercom system in the Islander at that time was always live so that one could converse without having to press a microphone button and as we took off I told the girl what I was doing and she listened to my calls to air traffic control. Soon after this she realised she could also talk to me and from then on I couldn't get a word in edgeways.

By the time we were abeam Wick I was getting very tired of the continual chatter and was wondering how to politely get her to shut up when a grinding noise followed by a loud bang came from the starboard engine, the revs dropped rapidly, the engine started to shake and I very quickly shut it down. I called air traffic control to advise them that I had an emergency and set course for Kirkwall in Orkney, the nearest place to my position, and also our nearest engineering base. Flying the Islander on one engine was no problem especially when as lightly loaded as we were so I wasn't particularly worried and relaxed as the adrenalin left my system. I then realised that there was a blessed silence in my headphones and the nurse never said another word the rest of the way to Kirkwall, a somewhat drastic way perhaps to quieten a chatterbox.

By the beginning of April two events took place, the first and most significant being that finally everything was ready for the licence to be granted for the airstrip at Unst and the flight operations inspector from Edinburgh told me that we could start our schedule service operation on 9th April, provided that the fire engine had been taken from the county council depot in Lerwick, where he had inspected it, up to Unst to the airstrip. This seemed straightforward and we announced that the first flight would be on the morning of the 9th and soon had all the seats booked in both directions. The other event was a phone call from Fetlar to say that they were just completing a very small strip 1,200 feet long and 30 feet wide and it would be finished by the second week in April.

On 5th April I flew the aircraft to Glasgow for maintenance, returning north on the 8th to find that the county council did not find it convenient to send the fire engine to Unst and that the start of the service would have to be delayed. I rang up the Commanding Officer of RAF Saxavord in Unst to tell him that everything was off and that the inaugural flight, on which he was a passenger, could not take place. When he heard why he immediately offered to provide fire cover with the RAF fire brigade if this was acceptable to the civil authorities. At that time the whole of the Scottish inspectorate was made up of men led by Donald Kirk who firmly believed that they were employed to help the development of aviation in Scotland and permission was rapidly forthcoming, so next morning we started on schedule as announced. The official fire engine arrived two days later. This was the first of many occasions when the RAF came to our assistance over the years and I am eternally grateful to all the Commanding Officers concerned.

The next week, on the 16th, I summoned Dennis once more and at 17.08 we touched down on Fetlar for the first time. The strip was on an excellent site and, though very rough and in need of more work, was acceptable for ambulance flights and I advised the medical authorities accordingly.

One day soon after this a chap came to see me and introduced himself as Derick Herning, a language teacher at the secondary school in Lerwick, and also local co-ordinator for the International Voluntary Service whose members, mostly students, were prepared to help with such projects as building community airstrips. I accepted his offer with joy and quickly organised groups to work in Papa Stour and Fetlar. Their transport and support had to be paid for and so I started on the first of my drives to fund the airstrip programme. Loganair's parent company at that time was the Royal Bank of Scotland and they, with great faith, agreed to provide the cash against the day when I could find it from other sources. The county council were still very reluctant to involve themselves though several councillors, notably Edward Thomason and Alex Morrison, were very supportive; the county surveyor at that time, Jack Moar, also gave me a lot of very unofficial assistance.

G-AVRA's first landing on Fetlar . . .

. . . but with no room to turn around the plane had to be pushed back to the end of the strip before being able to take-off again.

Photos: © Dennis Coutts

My search for funds led me to many odd corners. A fund that had been set up by Salvesen, to aid redundant whalers, provided some as did a dormant air ambulance fund which had existed from pre-war days; local business interests also chipped in but as this was still only a small start I approached the Highlands and Islands Development Board. At that time one of the permanent board members was Prophet Smith, a local man from Bressay, and I approached him initially; he referred me to the transport officer, Donald McCuish, and promised all possible assistance.

The major problem was that in order to get funding from the board the community in question had to raise at least 50% of the cost themselves, an impossible task for a small community. So a formula was evolved to overcome this difficulty whereby the labour put into the strip at local level would be credited at current labour rates. This was the first of many helpful decisions the board made. With funding now available and volunteers anxious to come and help plans were made to improve both the Papa Stour and Fetlar strips during the coming summer.

The scheduled service was now operating on three days a week and passenger loads were building up to the extent that we announced an increase to five days per week from 1st June.

About the middle of May a Norwegian fishing boat had a bad accident when a wire rope broke and the Norwegian authorities arranged that I should do two ambulance flights to Bergen so that the victims could be treated in their home country. The flight over took about one hour twenty minutes, adding meaning to the old story about Lerwick's nearest railway station being Bergen. This was the first of many flights to Norway over the years.

Ambulance flying, which we had expected to be a regular feature of our Shetland services, was very slow to start. Indeed I had only done two within Shetland since I arrived. There seemed to be a strong local resistance to it, as one person was heard to say: "People have been dying on the ferries for years without anyone making a fuss." Orkney, however, was different in outlook and I made several ambulance flights for the Orkney authorities during that summer.

As we moved on into June the foggy season started and on the 22nd I got stuck overnight in Unst. This started the critics: "You will never cope with the weather here and it would be better for the council to develop a better ferry service." It did however give me a chance to call on several people in the island and I found them all very enthusiastic for the aeroplane. The local doctor also confirmed that there was official resistance to him using air ambulances even

The Islander ready for take-off at Baltasound. The hut behind the Morris Traveller contained the fire-trailer and the coin-operated telephone used by the pilot in bad weather to contact Tingwall when checking on weather conditions there before take-off.   Photo: © R. Manders, 1973

14

though the Scottish Home and Health department who actually paid for the flights left it entirely to the discretion of the local GP.

In discussion with local businessmen I found that at the time there were only three mail deliveries a week in Unst and so started a system whereby urgent mail for them could be addressed c/o Loganair at Sumburgh and I would take it up on the next service for a small charge. This arrangement worked well for the next two years until Unst got daily deliveries and as the service grew to serve other islands it was extended to each one in turn. One amusing use was that island ladies who suspected that they might be pregnant and didn't want the fact to be public yet used to send the necessary sample to the pathological lab via the aeroplane rather than posting it at the island post office!

Next morning when the fog lifted I returned to Sumburgh and as if to confound the critics, though we were not always on time, this was to be the only weather cancellation of that first year's scheduled operations.

Chapter Three

As we entered July I was beginning to feel that progress was being made on most fronts. If I could only break down the resistance to the use of the aircraft for internal air ambulance flights I felt that the airstrip programme would take off. Two events in rapid succession were to do this in a dramatic manner.

I had just landed after the afternoon service to Unst when the control tower called me to tell me not to put the aeroplane into the hangar as there was an emergency in Foula. I started to refuel it whilst the airport firemen installed the stretcher and in about seven minutes my logbook shows I was airborne again with a local volunteer who had first aid experience coming along to act as nurse.

On arrival in Foula we found the district nurse down at the strip with a young man who was holidaying on the island. He had put his arm through a glass window and was bleeding very severely and only semi-conscious. She had found him collapsed by the roadside trying to reach her house and had done her best to staunch the flow of blood, but he had lost a very great amount. The flight to Foula normally took about 14 minutes and some 38 minutes after leaving Sumburgh I was landing back there to be met by the local doctor and ambulance from Lerwick. The patient was given an immediate blood transfusion and was soon on his way for the 40 minute drive to hospital, underlining the urgent need for a strip at Lerwick near to the hospital.

This flight got a lot of publicity both locally and nationally as without the rapid reaction with the aircraft the youth would almost certainly have died. The local hospital authority also accepted this and almost immediately arranged to store a variety of emergency medical equipment at Sumburgh so that it could be loaded into the aircraft along with the stretcher and such things as transfusions could be given in flight. They also arranged a volunteer rota of nurses from the hospital who would be willing to go on flights at short notice, and to cover the really urgent cases where we could have an unacceptable delay awaiting a nurse from Lerwick they agreed that the district nurses could also be called on.

It has always been a tradition of the Scottish Air Ambulance Service that the nurses are volunteers, their main reward being the granting of the right to wear the silver wings of an air ambulance nurse after successfully completing ten flights. The nurses show great devotion and courage in going on flights, often in weather conditions far more severe than they would ever experience on a normal passenger flights, at the same time having to cope with often severely ill or badly injured patients in what are rather cramped conditions.

When fitted up for an ambulance flight the Islander has a stretcher fitted down the left-hand side of the cabin, a seat for the nurse on the opposite side and two seats for additional attendants or relatives at the rear. The rest of the space is occupied by oxygen bottles, drip stand, resuscitator, anaesthetic equipment, etc., so that life can get quite hectic in the event of active nursing being necessary.

Only two days after this event I landed back at Sumburgh late in the afternoon just as the fog was beginning to roll in. Thankful that my day's work was over, I put the aeorplane into the hangar and after completing the day's paperwork went home for supper. About 8.00 pm I received a call from the Lerwick hospital to say that the County Clerk had been taken so seriously ill that they wished him flown to Aberdeen as soon as possible. BEA had said that because of the fog they were unable to fly the regular ambulance plane up from Glasgow and could I possibly do the flight. I said okay. I would be able to take-off and arranged to leave just as soon as the patient could be got to Sumburgh. I returned to the aerodrome and with the firemen's help filled the aircraft full of fuel and installed the stretcher. I then went up to the contol tower to check the weather in Aberdeen and likely diversion airfields in case the fog precluded a landing in Aberdeen.

At that time there was a strong lobby in official circles in Shetland who believed that the answer to all the problems of transport in the island could be solved by the use of big helicopters and there had been some correspondence in *The Shetland Times* to this effect. At this moment they went into action and at about 9.45 pm, when I rang the hospital to find out what was delaying the arrival of the patient, I was told than an air ambulance had been over-ruled and that a surgical team was to fly up from Aberdeen to operate on the man in Shetland. I politely expressed my doubts as to the ability of the helicopter to land as the visibility was by then down to 25 yards but was told that they knew better and that the helicopter would come overhead and just hover down through the fog, a popular misconception widely held in Shetland at that time.

As I was by now certain that the helicopter would not get in I remained in the control tower to await events. These were a long time in taking place as the machine did not leave Aberdeen until well after midnight, by which time the patient would have been in hospital in Aberdeen had the original plan been followed. Some two hours later the helicopter arrived overhead at Sumburgh but visibility was by that time non-existent and the whole of Shetland was fog bound. The captain very quickly decided to return to Aberdeen as a landing was clearly impossible. I still consider it was very irresponsible of the helicopter operators to have said they could carry out this flight in the first place as nothing in either the existing conditions or the forecast held out any hope of success and the only result was many hours delay for the patient.

The problem was now thrown back at me and whilst the weather was far below the legal limits for a take-off I knew that I could safely do so and in the circumstances felt justified in technically breaking the law, a decision I would not have had to take four hours earlier when the then legal minimum was still available.

I was airborne at 04.50 after having had to be guided out to the runway and helped to line up on the centre line by the airport firemen as I could not even see the runway edge from the cockpit. I landed at Dyce one hour and forty minutes later and the patient was transferred to hospital where he was operated on but unhappily died a few days later. Whether or not those many hours delay were vital I am not qualified to say but the whole event got tremendous national publicity and many in Shetland felt they could make such a judgement.

Suffice it to say that these two events altered local thinking and from then on ambulance flights started to become increasingly common. July was a busy month and at the end of it my logbook shows that I had flown 75 hours and 35 minutes over a total of 144 sectors, a very heavy workload for a pilot who was

Little and large – the huge RAF Beverley from Farnborough, unable to land at Unst, arrives at Sumburgh. The little Islander came to its rescue by flying top secret naval equipment onto its final destination.   Photo: © Dennis Coutts

also doing administration and development work. However, I was enjoying it very much and while occasionally thinking that a break would be nice I took it all in my stride.

With the possibility of ambulance flights always in my mind I was never off duty and became very abstemious in my habits, the only break being the occasional night when the Kirkwall pilots agreed to cover for me.

As the strip on Foula was very marginal the islanders agreed that we should try and develop a better site about half-way up the island. This site was relatively flat and consisted of a thin layer of peat over boulder clay and if the peat was removed would provide a firm foundation to construct a good gravel strip. A team from the roads department, who were over on Foula on another job, did a highly unofficial survey for me which confirmed this. Funding was available and also the possibility of an IVS team encouraged the islanders to start work on the new site.

By the end of the year local pressure was growing for a strip near Lerwick. It was the key to a successful inter-island service and also to a fully efficient ambulance service. However, there still seemed to be a lot of official resistance and no-one could agree as to where it should be placed. Once more *The Shetland Times* correspondence column was full of letters mostly in favour; some doubt was expressed by the pro-air service lobby about the accuracy of the minutes of one council meeting, who were later proved to be correct. Those councillors in favour were very active in their support for Loganair and with their encouragement I started to look for a site that could be developed on the same DIY lines that were proving successful in the islands.

1970 closed quietly on the aviation scene and 1971 was something to look forward to. I opened it dancing the eightsome reel in John Mouat's farm yard to a somewhat inebriated tune provided by Peter Hutchison on his accordion at two o'clock in the morning.

My first flight of the year was an ambulance flight to Foula followed immediately by a charter to take the crew of the Foula mail boat back to the island as they were stormbound over in Walls. The aircraft was loaded to the doors with supplies and the Christmas mail for the island. As the people of Foula still celebrate Old Christmas on 5th January this was in plenty of time for their festivities.

January proved to be a stormy month and I was hard pushed to maintain the scheduled service. In addition BEA had many cancellations and I made frequent trips south with stranded passengers returning with the newspapers and mail.

A very interesting charter came along during the month when an RAF Beverley transport, which was making its last operational flight before the type was retired from service, decided that it would not be wise to attempt to land at Unst due to the age of the aircraft and doubts about the reliability of one of its engines. The aircraft was loaded with top secret naval equipment and I was asked to move the load to its final destination. The Beverley was a huge aircraft capable of carrying 70 or so troops, plus their transport, and on this occasion its huge cargo bay was packed with crates and boxes. It was clear that it would take many trips to empty it and as one particular item was too big to get into the Islander Ken Foster brought a Shorts Skyvan up from Glasgow for the awkward items. I then continued with the Islander taking 11 trips to empty the vast fuse-lage. The Beverley was so large that it was possible to taxi the Islander right under its tailboom and load direct from its back doors.

In Shetland I was operating the Islander aircraft regularly in more severe weather than the type, which was still very new, had previously experienced and weaknesses started to show up. The wind speeds were often in excess of the air-craft's minimum flying speed and this meant that one had to virtually fly the machine while still on the ground. I was lucky in ground handling in that the older members of the fire crew had been trained in the technique of catching an aircraft as it landed with no forward speed in these conditions by Captain Fresson's Scottish Airways when they operated De Havilland Rapides in the north. However I was caught out one day when, after landing, and with men holding onto each wing tip to make sure the plane did not blow over, I turned downwind to taxi back to the hangar. Immediately the wind caught the rudder, slamming it hard over so that it hit the stop and broke. This grounded me until the next day when a new rudder was flown up and fitted. After that I always fit-ted a gust lock to the rudder when taxi-ing. Very soon afterwards Britten-Norman produced a much strengthened rudder assembly.

On the small strips another technique was necessary in high winds as there were only a few people available so that when I landed I had to keep the engines running, flying the aeroplane on the ground, until a truck could be parked in front of it for shelter after which I could shut the engines down and unload. In these conditions I never attempted to taxi. As the landing run was only a few yards I stayed put and when the aircraft was loaded up I restarted the engines and when ready waved the truck away and took off straight ahead.

At the beginning of February I learned another lesson about flying in remote places. I was asked to do an ambulance flight to Aberdeen late in the day when heavy snow was falling. Take-off time was uncertain as the ambulance

1971 and the first air ambulance flight using the Tingwall airstrip.　　Photo: © Dennis Coutts

bringing the patient down from Lerwick would have to be preceded by a snow-plough and also the airfield staff would have to clear a stretch of the east-west runway and keep it clear until I was able to go. At that time there were no night flying facilities at Sumburgh and in an emergency lighting was provided by gooseneck flares which looked like giant watering cans with a wick hanging out of the spout. The can was filled with paraffin and the wick lit. They were a relic of World War Two and were surprisingly effective although there was no illuminated centre line after take-off and, of course, as the take-off was to the west towards the sea no other lights for reference either.

The patient duly arrived and to avoid problems with snow building up on the wings we loaded her into the aircraft inside the hangar, then started up and taxied out to the runway. Luckily the snow had stopped by now but another worry was niggling away at my mind. Due to the patient's condition the doctor requested that the flight should be done as low as possible, preferably not above 500 feet. I reached the end of the runway, completed my pre take-off checks and, obtaining clearance from the tower, took off into the night. As soon as I was airborne I lost all visual reference due to the lighting situation and had a temporary and terrifying spell of total disorientation before I was able to establish myself on instruments. From then on I always made night take-offs entirely by reference to the blind flying instruments. The flight over the sea low down in total blackness was very tense and I was glad to see the Scottish coast near Fraserburgh show up as I flew into clear weather. When we landed at Aberdeen the patient was whisked away in a waiting ambulance and weather conditions still being bad in Shetland I decided to stay overnight in Aberdeen, returning to Shetland next morning. I was very pleased when about six weeks later the patient, now on the way to recovery, walked off the regular BEA flight and came into the office to say thank you.

In early March a possible airstrip site was found in the Tingwall valley and, while not ideal as it was six miles out of Lerwick, it seemed to offer the best chance yet of us getting a Lerwick airstrip. The very helpful airfield inspector from the Board of Trade came up and agreed that if the ground could be stabilised at one end and a rocky hump in the middle removed it could be made to fit licensing standards. I immediately applied to the HIDB for grant aid and early in April Prophet Smith announced that the board was withdrawing the offer of £34,000 previously made to the county council towards the cost of a Lerwick airstrip, which they still had no definite commitment to provide, and instead would make a lesser sum available to Loganair to develop a temporary strip at Tingwall.

With a possible site in view and cash available I put my mind to work to realise what everyone considered the key to a successful inter-island operation. Firstly, I negotiated an agreement with the Church Commissioners, the owners of the land, and with the tenant farmer, to allow its use as an airstrip. The Royal Engineers agreed to blow up and level the rocky hump in the middle as a training exercise, one of many community projects they have undertaken over the years. This removed a major obstacle in more ways than one and was completed in July. In the meantime the boggy area was stabilised by laying a woven plastic matting known as STOLMAT which when the grass had grown through would support the weight of a fully laden Islander and yet would not interfere with the normal grazing use of the field. What some archaeologist will make of it in future centuries I do not know.

Fire cover was a necessity for an airfield licence so two local crofters were recruited who would be able to stand by for aircraft arrivals and it was arranged for one of them to attend the Civil Aviation firemen's course at Stansted which he successfully completed. A fire trailer and Land-Rover were purchased and a small hut constructed at the side of the field, Finally, orange and white runway markers were constructed and the strip was ready. On 30th August I landed on it for the first time. While all major work was complete there were various small details still needed in order to satisfy the conditions of an aerodrome licence to enable scheduled as opposed to charter operations to be carried out and these were in progress.

Whilst all this was going on I also had to keep the regular flying going and with the increasing workload Captain "Barney" Baron came up from Glasgow and was trained on the island strips in order to come up and relieve me occasionally. At that time Loganair required all pilots to carry out six landings on each strip and then carry out two commercial flights under supervision before being considered qualified for island operations A total of 50 daylight landings were required before landing at a strip at night. This emphasis on careful training, implemented originally by Captain Ken Foster, the Chief Pilot, and supervised by Captain Bill Henley, the Chief Training Captain, was totally responsible for the unbeaten safety record of Loganair in those days.

By early June the new Foula airstrip was ready for limited use though not yet able to take a fully loaded aeroplane and towards the end of the month I made another little bit of history when I flew the Moderator of the Church of Scotland, Andrew Heron, out to conduct a service in the tiny church on the island, the first and as far as I know the only time the Moderator has ever visited Foula. Many of the small islands do not have a resident minister, the spiritual needs of the community being looked after by a lay missionary who frequently is also the school teacher, and this was the case in Foula. I know that this visit was a tremendous boost to the then incumbent as well as to the community as a whole.

In June we started a regular series of charter flights to Bergen on behalf of the Shetland-Norwegian Society. Links between Shetland and Norway were historical and had been strengthened during the war when the Shetland Bus was in operation and a lot of Norwegians escaping from the German Occupation to continue the fight against the occupier made their first landfall in Shetland. These flights were to continue for the next two years.

The scheduled passenger loads to and from Unst were growing and on some days extra flights had to operate in order to cope with the demand. The improvements to the Fetlar strip by the International Voluntary Service were completed in August and we added it to our list of charter destinations carrying out an ambulance flight to Fetlar from the new Tingwall airstrip to take a very old lady home after a long spell in hospital.

September started quietly but was to produce my second inflight emergency since coming to the Northern Isles. I had just taken off from Unst southbound on the morning schedule when I noticed that the starboard engine cylinder head temperature was rather high. This could be a gauge fault, not uncommon in aircraft, but in case it wasn't I climbed to 2,000 feet rather than the 500 feet at which I usually operated. An old aviation saying is that "height in hand is as good as money in the bank" and in case it was a real problem I felt that the extra height was a good idea in spite of comments from my more regular passengers about issuing oxygen masks due to altitude. At that time most of the passengers on the morning flight were RAF personnel going on leave and the aircraft was usually at maximum allowable weight.

By the time we were passing Lerwick the temperature gauge was entering the red sector and the oil pressure was starting to show a steady decrease, a sure sign that the problem was real and not just a gauge failure. I knew that I would have to shut the engine down in order to avoid damaging it and so was very glad of the extra height. I advised the passengers of what I intended doing, called the air traffic controller at Sumburgh to tell him that I had an emergency and gave details of the problem, and feathered the starboard engine. This stops it in such a way that the propeller is turned edgeways on to the airflow and becomes stationary thereby cutting down the drag caused by the dead engine. According to all the books the Islander was capable of flying quite happily at that height while fully loaded but this was the first time I had had reason to try it. I was much relieved to find that it would indeed maintain its height without even having to use full power on the remaining engine. Fifteen minutes later I landed at Sumburgh to the accompaniment of a full fire service turnout, which included the fast rescue boat out in the bay. I had a very relieved load of passengers and the beginning of a great faith in Britten-Norman's design which was last for the next 5,000 or so hours I was to fly the aeroplane.

The question of emergencies was always in my mind, especially so because at that time the Sumburgh airport control tower was only manned for scheduled flights and for air ambulance call-outs and during the largest part of the day when I was doing charter flights there was no-one to talk to on the radio. I got a lot of help at that time from Captain Jack Leask, a Shetlander, who on retirement from British European Airways as a senior captain had built a house on Ward Hill overlooking the airport at Sumburgh. He was very interested in the Loganair operation and listened in to all the flights on an airband receiver tuned to the airport frequency. He suggested that I should make all my radio calls when flying around the islands as though the tower was manned and he would log me in and out of all the airstrips so that if I did have a problem there was a good chance he would hear me and so be able to organise assistance. He would also telephone my wife to advise her of my ETA back at Sumburgh. He continued to help in this way for two more years until the coming of North Sea oil forced the Civil Aviation Authorities to go onto all day manning at Sumburgh.

Communications were not the only problem that I faced in those days as there was very little in the way of modern navigation aids in the north and no radar to assist in landing and no blind landing equipment of any sort at Sumburgh. Indeed for navigation purposes I still made use of CONSOL, a World War Two system installed by the Luftwaffe (German Airforce) in

Norway, and at that time still operational. It was a very simple system whereby a series of dots and dashes transmitted in a timed sequence identified one's position relative to the transmitter near Bergen. A change was then made to another transmitter in Northern Ireland and a similar check made. Transferring these two lots of data to a consol chart then fixed the aircraft's position to within a mile or two. I very soon learnt to recognise every rock and skerry around Shetland and all my flying was done visually, usually at very low level at about 500 feet but sometimes when the cloud was very low I might come down to 100 feet above the sea.

Weather information was another problem with very little local information available so I set up my own network of weather watchers around the islands. First thing in the morning I telephoned the Met Office in Kirkwall and spoke to the late Iain Nixon, a most experienced forecaster with many years of knowledge of the Northern Isles to his credit, who gave me a comprehensive analysis of what to expect during the day. He would also call me during the day if he saw any serious problems cropping up which he had not foreseen earlier. Next I would phone Mrs Mouat in Unst. She lived about half a mile from the airstrip and had a good view all round. "Can you see Saxa Vord (the highest hill on Unst and about 900 feet high) and is it clear of cloud?" If the answer was "yes" I knew it was all clear; if not I would ask if the hill to the south was clear and, finally, if that was also covered could she see the pier. If she couldn't see that I knew I would have to delay for a while. I did have occasional problems with the Shetland dialect as on the day when I was told that the pier was just visible but that it was a bit "asky". A quick visit to Jim Black in the BEA office next door led to the explanation that this meant that it was misty! Next I called the coastguard at Lerwick and checked the height of the cloud on Bressay and the visibility to the north and south of the harbour. Having collected all this information I would then decide whether to go or await an improvement in the weather.

Despite all these problems, by the end of the year I had achieved a regularity of 98%; in other words 98 out of every 100 planned flights had been completed successfully, though not always on time, which led to a scurrilous little story that was going around aviation circles at that time.

Aircraft: *"Sumburgh tower, could I have a time check please?"*
Tower: *"Roger. If you're Bealine its 12.15; if you're Loganair its Thursday!"*

Such regularity had not been achieved since Captain Fresson's Highland Airways had operated and it was ironic that in an aeroplane packed with up-to-date electronic gear we had to revert to his methods to achieve it.

With experience my weather watchers got so good on all the islands that eventually all I had to ask was, "Will I get in?" and they would say "yes" or "no". They were very seldom wrong!

As October passed we entered a period of severe gales which were to be a feature of the whole winter and I was hard pressed to maintain the schedule. Indeed unless the wind was in excess of 50 knots I stopped recording it in my logbook. Wind caused real problems on both Fair Isle and Foula as due to the hills and cliffs horrifying and indeed dangerous turbulence is experienced when the wind is from certain directions. After frightening myself on both islands I asked the company to put a restriction on landing on both of them when the wind exceeded 20 knots from the critical directions. This enabled us to operate safely to both islands for many years and it was only when these restrictions were ignored many years later that aircraft were damaged on both islands, though fortunately without injury to anyone.

Mrs Carrie Jamieson, a District Nurse in Unst, and Sister Margaret Manson of the Gilbert Bain Hospital, Lerwick, are presented with Silver Wings by Mr Robert Adair, chairman of the Shetland Health Board, in 1974. Silver Wings are presented to nurses who have taken part in ten or more ambulance flights. The presentation should have been made by Captain Whitfield but he was called out at the last minute – to make an air ambulance flight.   Photo: © Dennis Coutts

In addition to carrying out the schedules and local charters I still endeavoured to carry out newspaper and mail charters on days when the service from the south was cancelled due to weather.

One of the problems of high winds is that the Islander is a slow aircraft and high winds have a very marked effect on its ground speed. This can be illustrated by taking the case of an aircraft which cruises at, say, 300 knots flying into a 50 knot wind, its groundspeed will be reduced to 250 knots, a reduction of one-sixth, whereas an Islander flying into the same wind at a cruising speed of 130 knots will have a ground speed of only 80 knots, a reduction of more than one-third! Early in November I carried out an ambulance flight to Aberdeen into an 80 knot gale which took me 2 hours and 24 minutes to complete, rather more than the usual 1 hour 20 minutes. However, I returned to Sumburgh in 55 minutes!

In the meantime, all the formalities for the granting of an aerodrome licence for Tingwall had been completed and on 15th November I operated the first inter-island flight to use the new strip. This was a great step forward.

The gales continued unabated during December and the Foula mailboat was unable to cross to the mainland so that by Christmas supplies were running short and no mail had been received either so the islanders asked me for help. A large load of essential supplies was delivered to Sumburgh and the mail was sent down to Virkie Post Office in case there was a break in the weather. On Christmas Day the forecast promised a short lull in the gale so we loaded the aircraft and as soon as the wind had dropped to a safe level I made the 12-minute flight over to Foula, landing safely and quickly returning to Sumburgh for a somewhat late Christmas dinner. It was on the national news that evening as the only delivery of mail in the whole of Britain on Christmas Day.

A week later I made the news again when on the last night of the year I carried out an ambulance flight from Unst making the first ever night landing at Tingwall with a lady already well advanced in labour who was safely delivered soon after her arrival at the Gilbert Bain Hospital in Lerwick. Apart from some problems caused by a breakdown in the telephone system, which meant driving round the houses to collect the fire crew, the flight was routine on a fine clear night. Nursing attendance was provided by the Unst district nurse Mrs Carrie Jamieson, who was later to become the first district nurse ever to be awarded Air Ambulance Wings.

So ended 1971.

Chapter Four

January 1972 started off with a day or two of calm weather but by the second week I logged "wind 150/45 gusting 60" and we were back into the storms. I made my first trip to Stavanger since coming to Shetland into the teeth of this gale. It was a very weary trip over but we came back at jet speed with a tail wind which had by then risen to 100 knots!

The trip was to take council officials over to arrange the purchase of some Norwegian timber houses to be erected at Scatness to accommodate the rapidly increasing local population as the oil boom started to make itself felt. This necessitated me waiting for a couple of hours while the officials completed their business and, as it was lunchtime, I went to the airport restaurant to get something to eat. As I approached the door my arm was taken by a Norwegian who asked "Shetland?" "Yes", I replied. At this point he shook his head whilst pointing at the door and led me off to the staff canteen where he announced to all and sundry "Shetlander", the rest being unintelligible as I do not speak Norwegian. He then led me to the counter giving me a menu, also in Norwegian, and pointed to an item on the list again saying "Shetlander". He then disappeared. The waitress appeared a few minutes later with a dish of salt fish and potatoes, compliments of the house, so even though it is not my favourite dish I tucked into it while expressing my thanks. Two other men then joined me and explained that the first one and several other airport staff, including themselves, had spent time in Shetland while serving in the Norwegian forces during the War. They had all frequently been served salt fish whilst enjoying Shetland hospitality at that time and seemed to regard it as a sort of national dish!

On the 15th of the month a BEA Viscount inbound to Sumburgh reported sighting a ship's lifeboat to the north of Fair Isle and the Coastguard asked me to investigate it. Trying to find a small object in a vast and stormy sea without the aid of radar is not easy but as a vessel was currently reported missing in the North Sea the Coastguard was anxious to check it out in the limited time available before dark and it was obviously much quicker to use the Islander, which was on the spot, than await the arrival of the RAF Shackleton which had been summoned from Kinloss. We found the boat just as the light was fading and flying very low over it were able to see that it was empty. We also got a good description of it so that on checking back the authorities were able to establish that it did not come from the missing vessel but from an oil rig supply ship that had reported it lost a few days earlier.

The gales continued to such an extent that by the end of the third week in February the people of Fetlar, who were still dependent on the *Earl of Zetland*

and a flit boat to land supplies, were running short of some essentials so the owner of the shop there chartered the Islander to restock his shelves. This was the first time that the extended strip proved its worth as I was able to carry a full load into the island.

In February I also carried out a difficult ambulance flight to Papa Stour. I had landed at Tingwall on the way south on the afternoon schedule to find a message awaiting me to ring the office at Sumburgh (this was before we had a direct radio link between the aircraft and the office). On doing so I was told that someone had been injured on Papa Stour and that a nurse was on her way out to Tingwall from the hospital in Lerwick to go with me to collect the patient. At that time of year the service was timed in such a way that we left Tingwall just before it was officially dark at about 15.45 as we were not allowed to operate schedules in the dark. This meant that there would not be much light left by the time I reached Papa Stour and I anxiously awaited the arrival of the road ambulance with the nurse from Lerwick. Stanley, the airfield attendant, was laying a flare path for me at Tingwall as it would be dark by the time I returned and as soon as the nurse arrived we set off.

The flight to Papa took about eight minutes and it was very murky indeed as I started an approach with the windsock standing out stiffly at right angles to the strip showing a nasty crosswind with much turbulence on the final part of the approach. They had no flares on the strip but the white runway markers constructed the previous summer showed up well in the landing lights, which on the Islander are very powerful, and I was able to complete the landing. Three minutes later we were on our way back to Tingwall and 25 minutes after leaving Papa Stour the patient was being carried into the Gilbert Bain Hospital. Before the airstrips were built such a trip would have taken two-and-a-half hours, assuming that a boat could have made the crossing in the prevailing conditions.

The search for oil was beginning to gain momentum rapidly and its effects on the airport at Sumburgh were being felt in many ways. Loganair was able to benefit from the increasing activity to such an extent that it was decided that I should get a second pilot based in Shetland to help me. At Sumburgh there was no handling or customs agents and only one Telex machine which was in our office. Telephone lines were also in short supply as the GPO struggled to catch up with the increase in activity. Accommodation was also extremely limited though we were no longer occupying the old wartime buildings as a new purpose-built, though already too small, building had recently been opened.

With all this in mind I decided that Loganair should cash in on the situation, and having more staff to work both in the office and on the tarmac, went into the aircraft handling business as a sideline to our rapidly increasing flying operations. In due course this was to grow to employ a staff of 12 people and continued until expansion of the available facilities opened up the way for the big boys to step in and take over.

As we had the only supply of Avgas on the airfield we also became increasingly involved with aircraft refuelling and found ourselves having to ship in hundreds of barrels of 100 octane fuel. Most of the oil support was being done with piston-engined aircraft such as the DC-3 and the normal uplift of fuel would be about 300 gallons although one aircraft, which was doing long range survey work, required about 1,100 gallons per day. The refuelling was done by Andy Mainland, nicknamed "Brewsie", using an old ex-RAF bowser which held 1,200 gallons so that a lot of time was spent each day pumping barrels into the machine and whenever he had nothing else to do Brewsie, helped by Angus Goudie, a young chap who had just left school, would ensure that the bowser was kept full.

One day a DC-4 arrived from Norway. This was a much larger four-engined aircraft and we hadn't previously refuelled one. Brewsie positioned the bowser under the left wing, connected up the hose to the outer tank and started pumping. About 20 minutes later I looked out of the window to see how they were getting on and saw a worried-looking Brewsie looking into the pumping mechanism so I went out to see what the problem was. "It won't pump and I can't find out why", greeted me. I looked too and couldn't see anything obviously wrong so I asked if there was plenty of Avgas in the tank. "Oh, yes. It was full when I started" was the reply. At that moment light dawned on me and I suggested a check be made. On dipping the tank it proved to be empty, the aircraft having swallowed up all 1,200 gallons and went on to take another 800 before it was full. On checking we found that as fast as fuel was being pumped into one tank the aircraft's own flight engineer was transferring it to other tanks in order to keep the balance right. It was some days before Brewsie lived that one down!

This refuelling operation soon became full-time, and very profitable, and it was not to be many months before the island's main fuel distributor realised what he was missing out on while previously he had refused to have anything to do with the retailing of Avgas. He now exercised his rights as the holder of the airport fuel concession and took it from us. This was the first of many blows that the coming of the oil boom was to deal us as not only did we lose the profit on the fuel sales but, more importantly, we now had to pay retail rates for the fuel we used in our own aircraft. The airport authorities similarly jumped on the bandwagon with savage increases in our landing fees and hangarage and without the extra income we were generating from non-flying parts of our operation the scheduled service would have been in some danger.

The gales continued well into the spring, keeping me very busy with extra charter flights and in April Captain Jens-Peter Knudsen, a young Norwegian pilot who had been working for Loganair for about two years as a co-pilot and had just qualified as a captain, arrived to share the burden of the ever-increasing workload. Pete, as he was known, was to become a tower of strength in the next few years and was very popular in Shetland, not least because of his prowess as a piano player. He was much in demand at parties and, being single at that time, was also very popular with the young ladies.

My first task was to train him in the ways of operating in the Shetland environment and to qualify him on all the island airstrips. While doing this we had a particularly nasty experience. We left Sumburgh north-bound on the afternoon schedule with the inevitable gale blowing at close to our operating limit. I was flying the aeroplane and Pete was riding with me to see how it was done. We reached Unst in quick time with the wind behind us and got airborne again as quickly as possible as it was obvious that the gale was getting even stronger. Just north of Lerwick I realised that the wind was now too strong to risk landing at Tingwall, where there was not enough staff to catch and hold the aircraft, so we advised Sumburgh air traffic control that we were diverting direct to Sumburgh. The controller told me that the wind was now gusting to 70 knots and increasing and that he was organising at catching party to be ready at the runway intersection. We continued south with a groundspeed of around 40 knots which meant that it would take at least another 20 minutes to reach the airfield.

We passed through the harbour at Lerwick, flying at about 300 feet as the cloud base was lowering rapidly, and as we passed the south end of Bressay, always a turbulent spot, the aircraft seemed as though it had come to a full stop in the air, it shook and shuddered, we were all thrown hard against our seat belts and, for what seemed an age, the engines banged and spluttered. Then it was passed and we were moving forward again in relatively smooth air. I then realised that the controller was calling us very worriedly on the radio. He sounded very relieved when I answered and he asked if we were okay. I replied that we seemed to be and he then told me that for about three minutes the wind had exceeded 120 knots and that quite a lot of damage had occurred around the airfield.

We landed with the wind still blowing at 75 knots and with the aid of the catching party got the aeroplane safely into the hangar. On examining it carefully I found that the tailfin had flexed so much in the turbulence that the attachment points between the fin and the fuselage had been bent. An engineer and a spare aircraft had to be flown up from Glasgow to keep us in operation whilst our own was being repaired. Luckily Pete was not put off by this experience and by the beginning of May was to take his turn with the flying. From then on it became possible to get regular time off and also to spend more time on developing other aspects of the operation.

The gales gave way to fog and it was with some trepidation that I was wakened one morning in the early hours by the telephone. It was the doctor who served Foula to say that a man was very ill and could we go in and bring him out. I was relieved to see that the fog had lifted into low cloud and we quickly prepared an aircraft. The doctor lived in Walls, the nearest point to Foula by sea and the normal port of call for the Foula mail boat, so that traditionally the Walls doctor looked after the needs of the islanders. However, it was normally a good hour's drive from Sumburgh in those days and I was amazed when some 40 minutes after the initial call Dr Ditchburn arrived at the airport. I took off immediately he arrived hoping that there would be a glimmer of daylight to find the island as this would be my first night landing on Foula. The first hint of grey was appearing on the eastern horizon when I spotted the few flares which were available to light the strip and the landing was straightforward. We were quickly on our way to the man's house where, after the doctor had prepared him for the journey, the patient was loaded onto a trailer and taken up to the strip and so to hospital.

Early in May the people on Whalsay decided that they too would like an airstrip so I went over on a fishing boat specially sent to collect me and found a suitable site. I was then entertained to a most enormous tea by my hosts and, despite opposition from the local councillor (not a Shetlander), the population would get a strip at the earliest possible date. This began a very happy relationship with many fine folks on Whalsay and by late September I was able to land there though not yet able to add it to the scheduled service network.

May also saw the completion of licensing formalities for the Fetlar strip and on the 25th I flew the first scheduled service to the island. We were now operating Sumburgh-Tingwall-Fetlar-Unst twice daily and, on the two busiest days of the week, an extra flight direct between Sumburgh and Unst as well. The service operated a little like a bus, the pilot carrying a ticket machine and collecting the cash at each stop. We would carry anything which we could get into the aeroplane though Pete was a little unhappy about sheep as he was somewhat allergic to them.

At the beginning of June I received an ambulance call to Fetlar at one o'clock in the morning. At that time of year it doesn't get properly dark in

Souvenir covers commemorate the first scheduled flights to Fair Isle and Fetlar. The Fetlar cover was flown to Unst, transferred to Fetlar, where it was posted, then delivered to RAF Saxa Vord, Unst. The stamp cancellations are interesting as they show firstly the 25th May, 1972 "Fetlar Shetland" date stamp, then 30th May, 1972 "Haroldswick Unst Shetland" has been struck on the reverse together with the "RAF Post Office Saxa Vord Shetland" handstamp, and finally the "Loganair Sumburgh" boxed datestamp on 1st June, 1972.

Shetland and as it was a clear morning I climbed to about 3,000 feet en route, thereby seeing the sun rise as I climbed, then seeing it apparently set again as I descended to land on Fetlar, and then to rise once again after take-off for Tingwall.

We were again having problems with fog at Sumburgh even though by now the navigation aids had improved and there was talk of radar being installed. We found that the Tingwall strip was often fog-free when Sumburgh was "socked in" and this enabled us to do quite a lot of flying around the islands when otherwise we would have been grounded. New equipment, when it arrived, would be of great help to our operations but in the meantime, learning from the old Shetland ways of boat navigation, I had developed a technique to help find places such as Fair Isle and Foula in poor visibility.

In the days of the Haaf fishing, carried out in six-oared boats known as sixerns, it had been necessary to row about 70 miles to the west, "rowing Foula doon" as one old man told me, and to remain at sea for three days. Very few if any of the sixerns had the luxury of a compass yet managed to find their way home again regardless of visibility. This was achieved by a careful study of the wave patterns generated around the islands by an experienced crew member in much the same way as the South Sea islanders used to navigate over vast distances by their knowledge of wave patterns. The presence of land creates disturbances in the tidal flow which can be felt over a wide area.

I spoke to Jerry Stout, at that time skipper of the Fair Isle mail boat *Good Shepherd*, about how they found the island in fog with no radar or direction finder and I realised that some of this ancient knowledge was still in use. I reasoned that if these disturbances in the sea could be felt in a boat there was a good chance that they would be visible from the air and this proved to be the

Jerry Stout (centre) and the crew of the *Good Shepherd*.

Photo: © Dennis Coutts

case. Over many flights, by careful observation, I found that it was indeed possible to see this disturbance caused by the tide flowing past the island from some five miles down tide. I reasoned that it was much easier to find something five miles long than the mere length of the small island so I obtained a set of tide tables and a tidal atlas to determine which way the tide was flowing at any particular time and then flew a course which would cross this tidal string rather than aim direct for the island. This gave me a greater margin to absorb any error in steering the course and as soon as I was able to spot the tidal string I would turn up tide and follow it until I spotted the island. I tried this several times in good weather until I had confidence in my ability to make it work and thereafter used the method whenever I had to find either Fair Isle or Foula in poor visibility.

This had an amusing sequel about a year later when mist and low cloud had stopped all flying from Sumburgh. We were having one of our regular inspections by a Civil Aviation Authority Flight Operations Inspector at the time and we were sitting in my office discussing various aspects of the inspection when a call came in from the doctor who served Foula. He advised that one of the inhabitants appeared to be having a heart attack and he was anxious to get across there as quickly as possible. I was by now confident enough in this method of navigation to be reasonably sure that I could find Foula so I told the doctor to get down to Sumburgh as fast as possible.

The weather was well below any legal flying limits and the presence of the inspector was an embarrassment as, while it was tacitly understood by the authorities that we did these things in emergency situations, I did not want to do so openly in his presence. I explained the situation to him and suggested that he took a walk for an hour or so in order to be off the airport whilst I was flying. He asked me how I could possibly find Foula in the prevailing conditions and I explained the tide string system. At this he said "I will officially go for a walk but as a practising pilot would love to come along unofficially to see how you do it." I readily agreed to this and as soon as the doctor arrived took off with the FOI sitting in the co-pilot's seat. The cloud base was just over 100 feet above the sea and the visibility about half-a-mile as I set course carefully checking the time to ensure that in the event of failing to spot the string I would not fly on past the island. Just before time was up I saw the disturbed water and, turning, followed the line of it till the island loomed up out of the mist.

Landing was no problem and after a rapid examination of the patient, an elderly man, the doctor decided he should go to hospital. I called the controller at Sumburgh on the radio to tell him this and to ask him to contact the road ambulance to ask it to meet us as Sumburgh as I wanted all the help I could get from the Sumburgh radio beacon for the return flight rather than chance finding Tingwall clear enough to land. After loading the patient we took off and 15 minutes later landed back at Sumburgh.

We returned to the office and made the inevitable cup of coffee. The FOI had not said a word since we landed and we drunk our coffee in silence. Some minutes later he shook his head and said: "If I go back to London and tell my colleagues what I have just seen they won't believe me!"

The summer continued to be troubled by fog and on several occasions we found ourselves operating out of Tingwall on the inter-island routes as Sumburgh was fogbound, but eventually the inevitable happened and Tingwall became fogged in when I was on schedule and I had to divert back to Unst where I was forced to remain overnight.

August brought a shipping strike to the whole country and the dockers also refused to work so that a huge airlift of supplies to Shetland became necessary. All sorts of aircraft, including the RAF, were called in to help and for a few days, whenever the Islander was not otherwise engaged, Pete and I joined in shuttling back and forth between Wick and Sumburgh carrying mostly animal feeding supplies.

Ambulance flights were now a regular feature of our operations and with Tingwall in use many of these flights landed there as its closeness to Lerwick saved a lot of road ambulance time and patient stress. Several of our ambulance flights were of a psychiatric nature and during the summer I had one that turned very nasty. As the patient came out of sedation en route to Aberdeen the nurse was attacked by the patient with a pair of scissors in an attempt to open the door and jump out of the aircraft. Luckily the nurse was a big girl who had been an Army nurse and she managed to get the patient under control, but thereafter we always carried two nurses on that type of flight!

Activity due to North Sea oil continued to increase and with Pete doing more of the flying I found I was spending more and more time on developing the ground services side of the business in order to cross-subsidise the scheduled service as the swingeing increase in airport charges imposed by the airport authorities had increased our operating costs by a factor of ten! An attempt was made to move us out of our hangarage to make way for more lucrative helicopters and it was only due to the goodwill of Bristow Helicopters that we were able to keep a roof over our heads. Soon after the helicopter companies built their own accommodation and just afterwards the CAA demolished the old wartime hangar that we had used since coming to Shetland and Loganair was forced to build their own hangar on the other side of the airfield.

In November I carried out the first ambulance flight from the new airstrip on Whalsay to take a small child, who had been badly burned, to the strip at Tingwall for transport onto hospital in Lerwick. Later in the month I did a similar job for the animal population when I flew the vet to Fetlar to go to the aid of a sick cow. Another unusual flight in November was to take five Shetland ponies over to Foula. Brewsie, our do-anything helper, built a set of removable stalls which would bolt together and attach to the aircraft floor fittings when the seats were removed, the ponies were then sedated by the vet and loaded in. Flying with them on board was a little odd as they started swaying from side to side soon after take-off and this gave a most peculiar motion to the aeroplane. The news of this flight spread and flying ponies became fairly commonplace and eventually we were to fly over 40 across to Norway and Sweden as well as to Fair Isle and Aberdeen.

December continued the year of gales and showed up one of the major problems of the Tingwall strip which was severe turbulence in south-easterly gales and we were forced to divert several times for this reason. I carried out nine ambulance flights during the month, three at night, and all in difficult wind conditions. Pete also did three including the last flight of 1972 which became the first flight of 1973 as he left Sumburgh before midnight returning about 0300 to find the rest of us well into the New Year celebrations - not so amusing when one is stone cold sober oneself.

Chapter Five

Life in Shetland wasn't all work. The people are very sociable and, provided one is prepared to take them as they are and join in wholeheartedly, a very enjoyable lifestyle can be followed. Christmas was always very hectic during the years I was in Shetland, merging rapidly into New Year, and then continuing in fits and starts until Up-Helly-A' at the end of January. Whilst all the island joined in, Up-Helly-A' is definitely a Lerwick festival and rather than an event could best be described as a state of mind entered into by the whole community.

I was very flattered to be invited by Peter Leith to join his Up-Helly-A' squad for one year. Apart from the main event of the Guizer's Jarl's squad, which accompanies the replica Viking galley until it is burnt following a spectacular torchlit procession through the streets of Lerwick at the end of the day, there are many other squads all of whom prepare a short performance which is usually a sarcastic comment on some local event of the previous year. This is prepared and the costumes made in great secrecy which, of course, gives an excellent excuse to consume the odd can of beer at rehearsals. After the galley burning all the squads tour the various venues in the town to perform their act. This continues until about six o'clock the next morning and the old and wise remain abstemious during the night in order to ensure that the whole programme is completed! My most enduring memory of the event is the weight of the torches (some of the fainthearted use a support consisting of an empty tin on a strap over the shoulder by which the end of the torch is supported but Peter said: "No real Viking would admit that the torch was heavy, so we will carry ours properly") and the tremendous heat which is generated by the hundreds of burning torches.

The last year I was in Shetland Peter was the Guizer Jarl and I was able to salute him on the morning of his great day when he stood in the galley on the pier in Lerwick by making a low pass over the harbour in the Islander and dipping a wing to him as I flew past on the morning service.

Fishing was a regular summer pastime and occasionally a winter one too when the weather was kind. Trout fishing was excellent but our favourite was sea angling from our boat, an activity that all the family could join in. The fish run very big in Shetland waters and record-sized ones were not uncommon; indeed my son Hugh held the record for both cod and haddock at different times.

We also did a lot of sailing, making regular trips to places such as Mousa and Fair Isle. As the family grew our boat became too small for us and Hugh and I set out to build a larger one. Following the sinking of a ship loaded with timber in the North Sea there had been a bonanza of brand new timber washing up on the beaches in Shetland. For a few days there had been scenes reminiscent of *Whisky Galore* as everyone salvaged what they would and hid it away from the customs officials. Hugh and I gathered our fair share and we decided that this would be the basis for a new boat and had it sawn into suitable sizes. I bought a glass fibre hull and we used this timber to fit out a motor sailer type of vessel with five berths and a large engine to cope with the fierce tides around the islands. She was ketch rigged, with tan coloured sails, and after a year of hard work (during which my younger daughter Tanis was unable to see out of her bedroom window due to the presence of the hull immediately outside) we launched her in the Pool of Virkie naming her *Freyja*. During the next few years we were to sail many hundreds of miles in her both around Shetland and down the west coast of Scotland.

There was a very active pony club and a growing interest in riding and as I had previous experience of riding and Tanis had her own pony I became very involved in that in a variety of ways from shoeing ponies to judging at the local horse shows.

Shetland is a naturalist's paradise and I spent a lot of time observing the wildlife taking part one summer in a daily survey of seabirds as I flew around the islands and amassed records which were used in the NCC record of the Natural Environs of Shetland, which was a careful attempt to establish the status of wildlife in and around the islands before the effects of the oil boom took effect.

Growing out of this I made four year's observations of whales and dolphins of which I published a summary which was the first record of these fascinating creatures in Shetland waters since the whaling stations had closed down in the Twenties.

1973 started well and Pete and I were very busy on the service also doing many charter flights as the oil boom started to build up. Indeed Loganair started to look at the possibility of basing another, larger, aircraft at Sumburgh to cope with the increasing demand.

In March I had to carry out a particularly difficult ambulance flight which would have been impossible without the co-operation of the RAF at Saxa Vord. I received a call at about 23.30 to say that a man in Unst had suffered a heart attack and the doctor wished to evacuate him to hospital in Lerwick as soon as possible. The weather was poor but not impossible so I agreed to have a go with the proviso that I would not try to land at Tingwall as with the state of the weather I was doubtful of attempting to fly into the valley at night and it would save time if the road ambulance came straight to Sumburgh to await my return.

It was a very dark night, with the cloud base at about 600 feet, as I set course northwards flying just off the coast maintaining my distance by watching the phosphoresence of the waves breaking on the rocks. It was clear enough to see the light beacon on Mousa and as I passed it I could see the lights of Lerwick ahead. I passed through Lerwick harbour, leaving Bressay to my right, and as I cleared the north entrance I could see the light flashing on the pier at Symbister on Whalsay so felt confident of reaching Unst without too much trouble. After passing Whalsay there were no more lights until reaching Unst and if it was very dark I would then turn east to track over the lighthouse on Out Skerries, from there setting course for Unst secure in the knowledge that I would pass to the east of Fetlar, so getting a clear run into Unst where a small light beacon some two miles east of the airstrip would give me guidance.

There was no air radio beacon on Unst at that time but limited guidance could be obtained from a maritime radio beacon on Muckle Flugga, the most northerly point in the British Isles, which lies about six miles north of the airstrip. I could only obtain a bearing from this beacon for two minutes in every six as it was one of a cycle of beacons which transmit in turn from various locations in order that a ship can take cross bearings for a position fix. This is fine on a ship with lots of time to plot the position but of no real value for finding the airstrip in an aeroplane. However, I had a highly unofficial arrangement with the lighthouse keeper that in a dire emergency he would switch the beacon onto continuous transmit by holding the cycling mechanism closed, thereby giving me a steady bearing to home onto. I was also able to use the distance element of a military navigation system TACAN which was installed at Saxa Vord thereby getting a continuous readout of my distance from the transmitter. The end of the runway on Unst was 6.2 miles from this beacon and by using a combination of these two systems I knew that I could reach the approximate end of the runway but not with sufficient accuracy to make an instrument approach hence the need to fly maintaining visual contact.

Soon after passing over the Out Skerries I realised that the cloud was getting too low to continue underneath so was forced to climb to a safe height. At about 1,000 feet I came out of the cloud into clear sky to see the most fantastic sight; there was an aurora that night which was particularly bright and the top of the cloud layer was bathed in a luminous green light. Whilst this was most spectacular I was not very happy about the brightness as I knew that when I finally descended into the murk below the cloud my night vision would take time to adapt.

At that time we could talk to the RAF controller at Saxa Vord so I asked him to implement the arrangement with the lighthouse keeper and soon my radio direction finder was pointing steadily towards Muckle Flugga enabling me to home in overhead and set course in an easterly direction until my distance measuring equipment tuned to Saxa Vord showed that I was approaching the six mile point. I then started to fly a curving path to the right holding the distance at 6.2 miles and descending to the lowest safe height at which I could fly on instruments without the danger of flying into the hill to the west of the airstrip. At this height I was still in cloud and eventually, when I knew I must be over the strip, I had to overshoot and climb back above the cloud.

As I passed over the strip I noticed a glow in the cloud which I assumed was the RAF fire engine shining its searchlight straight upwards and this was confirmed to me by the Saxa Vord controller calling me up to say that the fire crew had heard me pass overhead. He also informed me that the patient's condition had deteriorated rapidly and that the doctor was very anxious to know what I thought of my chances of getting in. I explained my difficulties to the controller with regard to the cloud base when I had no means of accurately knowing where the end of the strip was. At this another voice came on the radio and I recognised it as belonging to the senior controller who I knew quite well. He asked me if I was sure that I could identify the airstrip from above the cloud and I agreed to try so asked that once again if the fire engine would shine its searchlight straight up and fire off flares as I passed over. I repositioned myself to the east and approached again without descending into the cloud. I soon spotted the glow of the light and called for a flare. A few moments later it soared up out of the cloud giving me a positive position.

Whilst I was doing this the controller had been watching me on the large air defence radar which normally searched to the north and east for Russian aircraft. He now had the position of the strip marked on the radar screen and asked if I would like to try a sort of ground controlled approach with his very unofficial assistance. I agreed to this asking him to overshoot me one mile before I reached the coast if I didn't have visual contact. In the meantime the fire crew down at the strip passed on a weather observation giving the visibility at 1,500 yards and the cloud base at about 250 feet - it was going to be very tight!

I now repositioned to the east and, getting courses to steer from the radar controller, started to descend deciding that I would go down to 200 feet if necessary, lower than that would be hazardous unless I was in the clear beneath the cloud. At 300 feet the sea was just becoming visible so I continued down to 250 feet which put me just below the cloud. Visibility ahead was very poor due to a steady drizzle but with the radar controller giving me a continuous distance to go I continued. Out of the gloom the small light beacon on the island to the east of Baltasound loomed up and as I passed it I saw the glow of the searchlight on the fire engine and then the gooseneck flares along the edges of the strip appeared. I put down full flap and landed calling the controller as I did so in order that the radar and the lighthouse beacon could revert to their official functions.

We loaded the patient and a doctor and soon took off again for Sumburgh. The patient survived and the next day was transferred to hospital on the Scottish mainland. So ended what must be a unique event in three-way co-operation and probably the only time that a huge air defence radar has been turned round to provide a GCA approach!

Ambulance flying, or indeed any sort of emergency or search and rescue flying, has to be a very carefully balanced operation. Great care must be taken not to let the drama of the situation cloud one's judgement - indeed a healthy sense of fear is perhaps the single most useful attribute in these situations. There is no place for the steely-eyed and lantern-jawed character so beloved of movie producers; such a one would inevitably end up with a broken aeroplane, if not worse, and this is of no use to the patient who is lying waiting for the aircraft's arrival. I was always aware also of the nurse riding in the back and trusting in me to get her safely back to the hospital with her patient, and of my own family at home who wanted me back safely too. Every move had to be thought out ahead of time, a course of action decided on which would cover any eventuality, and a firm decision made, when the conditions were too bad, to turn around and try again later. This philosophy enabled me to carry out over 500 such flights safely, only failing once to complete one though in some cases I made two or three attempts before succeeding.

The rapid increase in oil-related work now made a larger aeroplane imperative and in July Jim Taylor and Roger Tribe, together with a brand new Trislander, arrived at Sumburgh and straight away launched into oil flying. Captain Bill Henley, Loganair's chief training pilot, arrived a few days later and started to teach Pete and me to fly it. The Trislander was a lengthened version of the Islander with a third engine stuck on top of the tail and is surely one of the ugliest aeroplanes of all time. It could carry 15 passengers very efficiently plus a good load of baggage and when the seats were removed it was an excellent freighter. It did not however have any toilet facilities and rapidly became known in the oil world as the "Bladderbuster". We found it very economical to operate and extremely versatile and its long cabin enabled many strange oilwell tools to be carried. Later in the year we also fitted it out to carry ponies and flew several loads to Norway and Sweden.

42

Manager of the Lerwick branch of the Royal Bank of Scotland Mr William Reid at Sumburgh when Loganair's new Trislander arrived in 1973. At that time the bank was the parent company of Loganair and Mr Reid was asked by his head office to commission Lerwick photographer Dennis Coutts to record the event.

The only cloud on the horizon at this time was that the islands council was still showing no signs of starting to produce a proper airstrip for Lerwick and the temporary one at Tingwall was very much affected by weather and turbulence. Other communities were keen, however, and a small group of islands to the east of the mainland of Shetland, called the Out Skerries, started raising funds to build a strip. I visited the Skerries and found a possible site which would be of the absolute minimum size for public transport operations though not big enough to allow a scheduled service. In one day the community of about 100 people promised £2,000, raised from various sources including public subscription, towards the project. Another appeal to Donald MacCuish of the Highland

and Islands Development Board, a long-time supporter of air services in his role as transport development officer, produced the promise of the remainder of the cost and Frankie Tait, the contractor who was rapidly becoming our airfield expert, was soon hard at work.

A new airstrip for Fair Isle big enough to permit scheduled services was also well on in the planning stage as the number of flights to the island was increasing at such a rate that it was clear that a regular service was soon going to be called for. The existing strip on Fair Isle was only 1,200 feet long and 22 feet wide and was a relic of World War Two, when it had been constructed as an emergency strip only. Whilst quite safe for use by the Islander aircraft in the hands of pilots trained for this type of operation it was somewhat limited by

Basil Thorn's photograph shows the Skerries airstrip under construction. It was taken following a week of continuous rain when the contractor had to temporarily withdraw his men and abandon the project to wait for the weather to moderate.

crosswinds and also by severe downdraughts and turbulence in certain wind directions.

A survey showed that by swinging the axis of the strip some 20 degrees to the south it would be possible to increase the length to 1,800 feet and the width to 200 feet, thereby making its use at maximum all up weight possible and also greatly increasing the number of days in the year on which it could be used. Very few strips are limited for take-off load in the north as there is nearly always a wind blowing down the strip which can be taken into account in calculating the maximum permitted take-off weight as the wind has the effect of shortening the take-off run thereby apparently lengthening the runway. However, landing is a different matter as one cannot assume that there will be a wind when you arrive at the strip and therefore must leave the departure point at such a weight that when having burnt off the en route fuel the aircraft will reach its destination at a weight at which it can safely land in the most disadvantageous wind condition that may prevail on its arrival. When Fair Isle was finally rebuilt it meant that the only restricted strip in Shetland was the one on Skerries as work then in

One of the first charter flights to Fair Isle. Left to right: Alan Whitfield, R. Burgess, A. Manson, S. Flaws, G. Flaws, Alexis Nicol and M. Mouat.   Photo: © L. Burgess

progress on Foula meant that by the end of that summer the strip there had also been lengthened and widened to full standards.

August brought another period of fog but as the Tingwall valley was proving remarkably fog free, and we had by now learned a lot about sneaking around the rest of Shetland very low down, Pete and I managed to keep the schedule going most days. We also did a lot of ambulance trips to Aberdeen as the young BEA pilots who were then flying the Heron ambulance planes from Glasgow were somewhat reluctant to operate in the manner that we had become used to. This did not apply in the case of the older pilot such as the legendary Eric Starling, who could teach us all a few tricks, but of course wasn't always available.

One particular flight of this nature comes to mind when, in order to carry out an ambulance flight from Orkney when the airport at Grimsetter was fogbound, I followed the road in from the sea on the west side of the island and was able to land on the old wartime runway at Skeabrae. Only by having an intimate knowledge of the area could this sort of flying be undertaken and in order to keep ourselves up to date on the local area we all operated at 500 feet on our local flights so that the area was well known to us from low level.

This period of fog coupled with the pressures put on operators by the more unscrupulous of the oil companies led to some of the marginal air charter companies, of which there were too many competing for the work available, taking risks that were unjustified and there were some horrifying incidents at Sumburgh as the charter operators attempted to keep flying in order to hang onto the work they had as there was always someone else ready to step in if they didn't. As the pilots were neither trained or experienced in this sort of operation it was nothing short of a miracle that no-one was hurt or killed at that time. On one of the worst occasions a DC-3 attempting to land on a runway which was not really suitable but which had a slightly better visibility than the one he should have used, actually touched the sea as he attempted to stay beneath the fog. This incident was witnessed by several people, including myself, who all held their breath until he made it safely onto the ground. Other aircraft landed very short of fuel, especially helicopters which parked themselves on hilltops and in fields often with not enough fuel left to take-off again until more was taken to them in barrels.

The authorities seemed determined to turn a blind eye to many of these incidents which led many of us to believe that an instruction had come down from above to get oil ashore at any cost.

Eventually one or two operators became so blatant in their ignoring of the rules that some action had to be taken and some air operators certificates were withdrawn and some others were prosecuted. Even so, whilst the reputable operators continued to fly in a responsible manner, the rules themselves were slightly changed to enable operations to continue in conditions which would have previously been unthinkable and incidents were to continue for another two years until Sumburgh was brought up to an acceptable standard for continuous use by larger aircraft.

The pressure to get on with the oil development led to the local population's amenities being ignored and the quality of life around Sumburgh rapidly deteriorated. Aberdeen Airport was closed at night and so helicopter operators started training at Sumburgh, leading to disturbed nights as helicopters practised hovering all night long at the north end of the airport close to the village and also doing training circuits at 200 feet over the houses. They avoided the south end of the airport as that was where the hotel was situated and many senior oil company and helicopter personnel were resident there.

Eventually local pressure built up to such an extent about this that something had to be done to put a stop to it and force the operators to accept the disciplines they had to obey at mainland airports. The local councillor, an airport employee, was reluctant to get involved so I was asked to try and do something about it as I had already been successful in preventing the extension of the runway from closing off the entrance to the Pool of Virkie, an important small boat anchorage. This problem was overcome by forcing a clause into the planning permission for the extension which required a new entrance channel to be built before the old one could be blocked. This was in the long run to be a great asset to the community as it led to a considerable improvement to the anchorage as well as making navigation in and out infinitely easier.

I therefore decided to approach the noise problem in the same way by organising a community objection to the planning application for the proposed new terminal buildings and hangars. Included in the objection was a clause stating that it would be withdrawn if certain safeguards were included in the planning permission including the stopping of unrestricted training and night hovering tests and the introduction of proper arrival and departure procedures to keep aircraft as far away from the inhabited areas as possible. This made me very unpopular with the major operators, especially the national helicopter company, who tried to bring pressure on me through my employer to withdraw from local politics. This made me more determined than ever to succeed and in the event we were largely successful in our aims.

The year was by now drawing to its close and on 19th December I made the first landing on the strip on Out Skerries. It was very tight to get into as approaching from one end it was necessary to skim over the lighthouse before making a steep descent onto the end of the strip whilst landing from the other end a similar steep descent over a rocky hill was required. With proper training it proved perfectly safe to use and has continued so to this day. It would not be available for regular use until the following spring when the new grass grew in but I was able to tell the islanders that we could now use it for ambulance flights if required.

On the 23rd I did my routine Christmas delivery to Foula then started the first real Christmas holiday that I had had in four years, not flying again until 6th January, so that for the first time since coming to Shetland I was able to join in all the festivities.

Here she comes! Skerries school children eagerly scan the horizon as Islander G-AXSS makes her first visit.
Photo: © Basil Thorn

Skerries air strip with the lighthouse in the distance.   Photo: © Ian Ray

Captain Whitfield in discussion with islanders on the new, hardcore strip on Foula in 1973.
Photo: © A. Gear

Chapter 6

The Seventies were a time of industrial strife in the north and somebody somewhere always seemed to be on strike or working to rule. This affected us in various ways - the dockers gave us an increase in charter activity as we flew in urgent supplies, airport baggage handlers disrupted normal operations and caused delays, and airport firemen closed various airports from time to time. We were fortunate in Shetland in that the airport staff belonged to a different union to the one which caused most of the strikes and so never had a shut down at Sumburgh but had several times to cope with problems at Aberdeen.

The worst of these occurred one night when I was called upon to do an ambulance flight to Dyce with a very ill patient. The airport there was being affected by industrial action at the time but as we could legally operate ambulance flights without full emergency cover I was able to fly in. In the event the airport firemen agreed to give the minimum cover necessary for the landing and all seemed to be okay. I arrived at about midnight and started an ILS approach as the cloud was very low. I broke cloud at about 350 feet and was given clearance to land. At about 100 feet and just approaching the runway all the airport lights went out plunging everything into total darkness. Luckily the Islander had superb landing lights and I could see the centre line of the runway whilst at the same time the fire engine turned on its big light so enabling me to land safely. I was told later that someone had cut the main power cable deliberately just at the crucial moment though who was responsible was never discovered. This was the only time ever that industrial action had a direct effect on an ambulance flight.

At about this time the unions decided to try and organise Bristow Helicopters, a move strongly resisted by the management. The unions brought all their guns to bear on Bristows in an attempt to stop them operating but with no success so the action was stepped up to include British Airline Pilots Association members who worked for British Airways thereby stopping all the scheduled flights to Shetland. This meant that many BA helicopter pilots who lived in the Aberdeen area and commuted home from Shetland via their mainline flights had to start asking the oil companies for seats on the oil charter flights in order to get home. At that time Loganair was providing the handling services for these flights out of Sumburgh and most of our staff were Shetlanders who felt somewhat aggrieved that Shetland life was being upset by a dispute which had nothing at all to do with the islands. They had a meeting and told me that as a protest they would not load any striking staff onto oil company charters unless they would have travelled on that particular flight in normal circumstances. This rapidly produced a phone call from the local BALPA organiser to protest that they did not want to be involved in the dispute but had been ordered to take action in London. I suggested that they all went back to work in that case and showed that they had minds of their own. This was followed by a call from the union secretary with all sorts of threats but as none of our staff were unionised they stood firm and no striking staff travelled until the dispute was settled with Bristows coming out on top.

A fuel crisis also hit the country at about this time and petrol came into short supply - indeed car owners were issued with petrol coupons but they were never actually put into use. However there was a marked shortage of Avgas and we had to severely ration what supplies we had which meant that we could only provide very small amounts for visiting aircraft, normally only enough to get them back to the mainland to the first available refuelling point. This was working out fairly well until a Danish Air Force DC-4, a large four-engined aircraft, was unable to land in the Faroes whilst en route to Greenland and was forced to divert to Sumburgh. His minimum fuel requirements would have kept the Islander flying for a week!

The Faroes, some 180 miles to the north west of Sumburgh, had a very poor weather record and aircraft frequently sat in Sumburgh for days waiting for fog to lift. We were called on to fly to Faroe from time to time and while the distance was a little too far for the Islander, due to the air navigation regulations covering engine failure and the availability of alternate landing grounds, the Trislander was okay as it had three engines.

Faroe had no instrument landing system or radar at that time and as the runway was on a neck of ground between a fiord and a lake with only one way in and one way out it provided an interesting problem. A cloud break was normally made using a radio beacon on a small island some miles away and one flew south west until sighting Vagar where the airfield lay. It was then necessary to fly along the cliffs, if the cloud was low, until a waterfall appeared. A left turn was then made to fly through the gap that the waterfall emerged from - this put one over the lake and part way along the lake a marker appeared to the left showing the way into the valley. Immediately on turning the corner the runway appeared in front. If unable to land one continued straight ahead following the fiord out to sea and started the whole process again. No wonder that the regulations demanded that one's first visit be in the company of an experienced pilot familiar with the place.

51

In the early part of the year I had a rather unusual experience. I am not a very religious person though a firm believer. On this day an ambulance call came in from Unst to go and collect a critically ill person and take him to Tingwall for transport to the hospital in Lerwick. Due to his condition special nursing and equipment was required and this would necessitate a landing at Tingwall on the way north to pick up two nurses and the necessary life support machine.

The weather was very poor with continuous snow and poor visibility but still above our operating limit. Pete Knudsen was duty pilot and was soon airborne. After about 10 minues he called us on the radio to say that visibility was zero and he was returning to Sumburgh. When he landed he told me that just to the north of the airfield the snow was very heavy and he had had to climb to a safe height and had been unable to find a gap into Tingwall. I never suggested to less experienced pilots that I should try when they had returned as I felt that this would not help their confidence and was not the proper way to run things but whilst discussing the situation with Peter he suggested that perhaps I should have a go. A call to Tingwall told me that the weather was still impossible but as the aircraft was full of fuel I decided to fly up any way and if necessary hold until it improved.

Almost immediately after taking off I found the same heavy snow that Peter had encountered and had to climb to a safe height and use the aircraft instruments to fly to the approximate area of Tingwall where I found conditions still very poor and so started to circle and called the office on the radio for a further weather check. They told me that the doctor from Unst was on the phone wanting to know what was happening as the patient was sinking fast. I knew that the situation was beyond me so started a short prayer to the effect that despite all the skill that God had given me if he wished the patient to live He would have to help me. Almost immediately a rift appeared in the driving snow and at the bottom of it I could see the strip and the ambulance waiting. By the time I had landed the snow had closed in again but quickly loading the nurses and their gear I made a blind take-off and some 15 minutes later landed at Unst. The return journey was equally dramatic and I was greatly pleased to hear the next day that while still very ill the patient was out of danger.

Ambulance flights were now occurring on average about three times a week, some of them carrying men injured on the rigs and onshore construction works whose injuries were sometimes pretty horrific. When doing ambulance flights it is important to avoid getting emotionally involved and to keep everything on an impersonal level but sometimes this was to prove impossible and I would find myself feeling very upset as a result of some of the flights, especially when carrying patients personally known to me or young children who had suffered avoidable accidents. Indeed one flight of this nature was doubly upsetting as it resulted in one of the very few rows I ever had with an air traffic controller.

I was called to take a child to Aberdeen one night who had been poisoned by drinking something that had been stored in a lemonade bottle and she was very ill indeed. On occasions such as that we signified the extreme urgency of the situation by adding to the normal flight plan "Request priority due to patient's condition" and this normally got an immediate clearance all the way. I had made this request on this occasion and all went well until I started my approach to Aberdeen. On being handed over from the approach controller to the tower controller and expecting a landing clearance I was advised that due to heavy helicopter training activity I should maintain 2,000 feet and join the circuit for a visual landing. This would add at least 10 minutes to my actual arrival on the apron and as I considered that time was vital to the child's survival I advised the controller that I must land immediately at which he reiterated his previous instruction. I there upon told him that I considered that the flight was in an emergency situation and that I was continuing my approach for a direct landing and that he should get the training aircraft out of the way. I could see two helicopters ahead of me and could also see that their pilots were already acting on their own initiative to give me a clear path and so was able to continue and land.

After seeing the patient safely on her way to hospital I was summoned to the telephone and following a very acrimonious discussion with the controller concerned was informed that I was to be reported for just about every air traffic offence in the book. I countered by telling him that I intended filing a complaint myself, which I did. I don't know what happened after that as I never heard anything more about the matter and continued to have a harmonious relationship with air traffic control for most of the rest of my flying career.

The child survived though she was in hospital for many weeks. Just recently I heard that she is now married and has started a family of her own.

In addition to being called on for ambulance flights from the various islands in Shetland and Orkney I was increasingly being called upon to operate from other destinations in the north of Scotland when the Glasgow aircraft was already engaged in a flight elsewhere and the flight was of an urgent nature. An patients from Wick, Inverness, Dounreay and even Stornoway. Indeed, on one busy day, accompanied by Sister Manson, one of the regular volunteers, I did three flights within Scotland before eventually returning to Sumburgh.

Had I known what 1975 was to bring I might well have cancelled the year before it started. The winter had been very wet and operating out of Tingwall was becoming increasingly difficult. Never an easy strip due to the approach through the valley, which was often subject to turbulence, the very wet weather had turned the surface into a bog causing a reduction in loads so that take-off could remain safe. In addition the surface was becoming very rutted and we were cancelling a large number of calls there. Also, as it was a public licensed strip, it was open to anyone to use and with the oil boom in full swing was being used by dodgy operators in unsuitable aircraft and at take-off weights which would have been prohibited under Loganair operating rules. One or two near disasters had occurred and I reluctantly decided to close the strip completely until the spring.

Soon after this the annual inspection for the aerodrome licence took place. During the previous year licensing standards had been tightened up and in order to renew the licence an exemption would have been necessary. With this in mind

Sister Margaret Manson on an ambulance flight from Foula.

Photo: © A. Gear

the authorities, who had always been a great help to us, felt that they were unable to grant a renewal, a decision with which I was in full agreement. The original licence had been a temporary one to enable us to operate until the islands council would have completed a proper airstrip to service Lerwick, at that time believed to be only 18 months away. Now some three years later there was still no signs of a site having been chosen let along work commenced.

Without a strip serving Lerwick passenger figures plummeted and the whole future of the service came under threat. Since coming to Shetland in 1969 losses had been steadily mounting but the Royal Bank of Scotland, Loganair's parent company at that time, had kept things going in the belief that once the service was properly established the Scottish Office would provide an operating subsidy to help the company break even on the inter-island service as they were already doing in other areas. The second blow fell in April when the Scottish Office announced that in future all such subsidies should be provided by the appropriate local authority, in this case Shetland Islands Council.

So began a period of backbiting and recrimination which did little credit to either the council or the company. Both took up entrenched positions, failed

Captain Whitfield after the suspension of scheduled services in October, 1975.

Photo: © Dennis Coutts

to get together to discuss the situation and slagged each other off in the press. I think the basic problem was that the company felt, and I think rightly so, that the service should be regarded as a separate entity which should stand on its own feet, whilst the council believed that the company was making a killing from the oil boom and wanted a subsidy to put "cream on the cake" as Col. Dainty, the councillor for Whalsay and never one of Loganair's friends, put it. In the short term this cross-subsidising might have been successful but as no one knew how long the boom would continue I believed that in the interests of ensuring continuity of the scheduled service it was necessary to get it on a firm basis as a separate entity, a belief that time has borne out as the oil boom as such died a relatively quick death.

Had the company put this view dispassionately to the council and been prepared to back it up by allowing access to the relevant accounts I think that the bitterness would have been avoided and the suspension of the scheduled service in October of that year would not have taken place.

In the meantime while this was going on we soldiered on flying, sometimes round the clock, to cope with all the work which was going on. In March I was faced with a particularly difficult night ambulance flight with a diver who had been brought in from one of the rigs by helicopter suffering from the bends. There were no decompression facilities available on the island and the doctors decided that he should be immediately evacuated to where a decompression chamber was available. The bends are caused by a diver surfacing too fast and not giving the gasses which are in the blood under pressure enough time to stabilise, the result being that bubbles form in the blood which is very painful and can result in permanent disability or death. Obviously the first treatment is to put the diver back under pressure causing the bubbles to dissolve and then to depressurise slowly. Flying was the quickest way to get him to decompression facilities but flying also meant lowering the surrounding pressure further so I was asked to fly as low as possible in order to keep this pressure decrease to a minimum.

Luckily it was a fine clear night and I was able to fly along quite safely at about 150 feet with the doctor in the back with the patient asking me to go lower and prudence suggesting that a higher altitude would be less nervewracking. At that time we often talked to the RAF radar at Buchan on the coast and they would give us what assistance they could. I called them and told them my problem and asked them to look out for me in the hope that they would spot me and give me a distance to go to reach the coast as at that very low level the DME in the aircraft would not lock onto the Aberdeen beacon to tell me the distance direct. Buchan saw me eventually when I still had about five miles to go over the sea and said that they would watch me in. Almost immediately after this the aircaft entered a bank of fog and safety demanded that I climb to a safe height for flight on instruments, in that area 2,300 feet. The doctor said that he doubted that the patient would survive this but there was little option. Luckly at about 400 feet we found ourselves above the fog and whilst the patient's comfort rapidly decreased the doctor felt that if we didn't go any higher he would probably be alright. I told Buchan of my problem and they agreed to steer me above the fog around the coast so that I could stay as low as possible. This they did and about 20 minutes later I was able to land safely at Aberdeen. The outcome of this and other similar incidents was that the oil companies developed a portable compression chamber which would fit on board a big helicopter and no-one was to be faced with this particular problem again.

The oil boom was having many other advantageous results for flying in Shetland and whilst we rather resented the curtailment of our accustomed freedom of the skies in the north we much appreciated the coming of better navigational aids especially when Sumburgh got radar for the first time and radar approaches in bad weather became available. One of the first ambulance flights that I carried out after the radar was commissioned would have been near impossible in the conditions prevailing if it had not been in service.

I received a call from the doctor in Yell asking me to go to Fetlar to pick up the district nurse who had broken her arm. It was a misty evening with a low cloud base and just getting dark as I took off and headed north. My intention was to pick up the patient and land her at Sumburgh where the ambulance would take her up to Lerwick. As the weather was dodgy I had a full load of fuel so that in the event of the weather closing in completely I could divert to Glasgow if necessary as the bad weather was affecting all the northern airports.

On arrival at Fetlar I saw that the cloud base was right down to the ground at the higher end of the strip but that the lower end was just visible. This meant a downwind landing but as it was only a very light breeze this was no problem and I soon had the patient on board and took off for Sumburgh. Soon I ran into fog and had to climb to a safe height. I called Sumburgh and was told that the weather there was rapidly worsening and in fact was almost below limits. At that time the radar had just been commissioned and there was only one operator qualified to operate it as the others were still under training and had to have a supervisor in attendance. As it was an ambulance flight for which the airport had been specially opened the supervisor was not there and the duty controller was not qualified and told me that the radar would not be available so I expected to have to make an older type of approach which was not as accurate and hence not usable in such bad conditions as one controlled by radar. With this in mind I started mentally planning for a diversion to the Scottish mainland. However, as luck would have it, the one qualified operator looked out of his window at home and seeing the airport lights on and the very poor conditions prevailing went down to the airport and got the radar warmed up.

By the time I started my approach the weather was very bad indeed and as I descended I began to doubt that I would see the runway at the half mile distance at which the approach using that type of radar terminated. As I approached the half mile the operator informed me that he could assist me no further but instead of stopping talking he continued to give me advice until, as I came to the end of the runway, I was able to see enough of the lights to enable me to land safely.

Whilst the oil boom brought an enormous number of advantages to Shetland it also destroyed, by a gradual process of erosion, many of the great attractions that the place had enjoyed in pre-oil days. A subtle shift in attitude set in amongst the population, especially the younger members. A more mercenary approach became obvious, neighbourliness decreased and old values were derided. I very much doubt that in the new attitudes prevailing the very great community efforts which had helped me establish the network of airstrips in the islands would have been forthcoming. I had arrived just in time to experience the older Shetland - I was not too sure that I was going to like the new one as much!

As the summer passed into autumn the dispute between the company and Shetland Islands Council became increasingly bogged down in entrenched positions and by the time a meeting was finally held between the two sides it was clear that any agreement was a very long way off and the company rather suddenly announced that the service would cease at the end of September.

Ironically the last scheduled flight proved abortive as when I reached Unst I was unable to land due to the onset of fog and had to take the passengers back to Sumburgh and put them on the ferry.

Other changes had been taking place in the organisation at Sumburgh. Peter Knudsen had been promoted to senior pilot and had gone to take over the Loganair base at Stornoway and Ian Ray, newly out of the RAF, had joined me in Shetland. Peter had been a tower of strength since coming to Shetland and I was very sorry to see him leave but Ian quickly proved that he had what it took to be a good "island pilot" and was eventually to become manager in Shetland.

The end of the scheduled service did not mean that flying stopped as there was a lot of charter work to be done and ambulance flights were almost a daily occurrence so that we continued to be busy. However, the local population were not pleased at losing something which had made life so much easier and the resultant fuss concentrated the minds of all concerned to such an extent that suddenly work started on preparing for a new airstrip at Tingwall and real negotiation started on the question of a subsidy.

November was busy and I spent a lot of time helping out in Orkney as they had a pilot shortage at that time. By the end of the month it looked as though progress was being made on the council front and in early December a temporary agreement had been reached so that we were able to restart the regular service before Christmas.

On the 23rd I did the now routine delivery of Christmas mail and supplies to Foula and finished 1975 with a night ambulance flight to Aberdeen.

Chapter Seven

The year started uneasily. We knew that the subsidy arrangement which had been made to get the service restarted was only a temporary one and all the staff wondered if there was sufficient goodwill to really get the service onto a firm basis. Much would depend on the timely completion of the new airstrip at Tingwall which we knew would make a vast difference to the passenger figures and therefore the greater viability of the operation.

In the meantime the council was still pursuing the idea of setting up its own operation to replace Loganair and what was worrying was that it was obvious that those who held our fate in their hands had very little idea of what was involved in the operation of an aeroplane as some of the comments made by one or two councillors revealed. Those that believed in the air service were very supportive, however, and whilst it is perhaps a little unfair to pick out any individual I must give thanks to two in particular, Edward Thomason and Jim Irvine, for their efforts on our behalf.

On the flying side I had a spate of ambulance flights in January and February, including six from Fair Isle, two of which involved the transfer almost immediately of the patients to Aberdeen. As the scheduled service was only running at a low frequency the aeroplane was more readily available to help out elsewhere and we did several ambulances out of Orkney and from Dounreay and Wick also.

One of those from Dounreay was particularly interesting as it involved the transfer of newly-born twins, who were suffering severe respiratory problems, to Inverness. The babies were in an incubator and attended by a doctor and a nurse who were very concerned by their condition as they were very blue in appearance and even to a layman appeared to be very poorly. As was normal with patients with breathing problems I was flying as low as was prudent even though the incubator was supplied with oxygen. About half-way to Inverness a sudden snow storm blotted out the countryside and I had to make a very rapid climb to a safe altitude for flight on instruments. As I levelled off at about 6,000 feet I was aware of a sudden burst of activity in the back as both the doctor and the nurse opened the incubator and each took out a baby. When I had the aeroplane settled down in the cruise again I looked around, fearing the worst, only to realise that both the doctor and the nurse had broad smiles on their faces and that clearly there had been a dramatic improvement in the babies' condition. When I landed at Inverness both were a healthy pink colour and it was clear were no longer causing as much concern.

After the ambulance had departed to the hospital we went into the airport building for a cup of coffee while the aeroplane was being refuelled. Then the doctor told me that the decrease in pressure caused by our rapid climb had apparently cleared the fluid, which was causing the problem, from their lungs and hopefully they would now make a complete recovery. This I am glad to say turned out to be the case. I presume the effect was much the same as was known to help victims of severe whooping cough by taking them up to a high altitude very quickly, something I had been called on to do once in the past when I worked in Canada.

At the end of March I went down to Glasgow for my six-month competency checks and became involved in a particularly difficult ambulance flight to Barra. I was in the ops room at Glasgow having coffee and a chat after completing my tests when a very urgent call came from the doctor in Barra. The regular ambulance plane was out on another call so the ops officer asked if I would do the flight. To this I agreed and started my flight planning. A call to Barra revealed that the cloud base there was very low and visibility was just about the limit; added to that the tide was coming in and as the landing ground on Barra is the beach and only usable when the tide is out it was going to be a race to get there first. The nurse arrived from the Southern General Hospital and turned out to be the legendary Sister Gisela Thürauf, probably the most experienced air ambulance nurse of all time and soon to be awarded gold wings for completing 500 missions. Later she also received the Queen's Commendation for Valuable Service in the Air, one of the very few women to be so honoured.

We were very quickly airborne on a priority clearance and climbing to 8,500 feet set course for Tiree where an instrument descent would be made using the Tiree VOR beacon before continuing low level the rest of the way to Barra which has no beacon and can only be approached visually. After leaving Tiree the weather deteriorated rapidly and soon we were flying very low indeed with forward visibility very limited. Due to the low level the signal from the Tiree beacon soon faded out and I was left with dead reckoning only to find Barra. This meant keeping a very close watch on the time and when I reckoned that I had another five minutes to go I slowed right down to minimum safe speed to ensure that I didn't fly straight into the side of the island.

Soon after I spotted a large green buoy which I knew lay off the coast a little to the south of the direct course to the beach so that as soon as I sighted the coast I turned north to look for the small island that lies at the entrance to the bay that contains the landing beach. I was in constant communication with our traffic girl in the Barra terminal who told me that she couldn't see the small island and that the tide was well inside the first two markers leaving very little dry sand available for a landing. I soon saw the island myself but the cloud seemed to be right down to the sea and there appeared to be no way in so I started a slow circle hoping for an improvement. The nurse, who was sitting in the co-pilot's seat, suggested that on a similar occasion in the past it had been possible to sneak in from the north so I flew on towards Uist to see if this was a possibility.

In the meantime the tide was still coming in and by the time that I found a gap between the cloud and the sea the radio reported that the beach was now covered. As I flew slowly along the shore towards the landing area I noticed that in the next bay to the north a narrow strip of sloping beach was still dry and it looked just about wide enough for a landing so when I reached the normal landing area and saw that was indeed completely covered I started a slow left hand circle back to the small dry beach and landed with a curving run and one wing well down on the sloping beach. Due to the sand dunes I was no longer in contact with the terminal so was unable to tell them what I had done. I then set off to taxi round into the proper bay to pick up the patient. This entailed having one wheel actually in the water and the aeroplane leaning steeply to the left due to the slope of the beach but in fact was not a difficult operation.

In the meantime at the terminal the ground staff had seen me enter the bay then turn away out of sight again, soon after hearing the engines apparently stop. Repeated attempts to call me on the radio failed and, fearing the worst, the crash wagon was despatched so that as I came round the corner I saw coming towards me a vast bow wave as the vehicle raced through the water. They were very relieved to see the aeroplane taxi-ing towards them and led me back to where the ambulance was waiting. We soon had the patient on board and using a similar dry patch at the other end of the beach for take-off were soon on the way back to Glasgow proving yet again the amazing versatility of the Britten-Norman Islander.

I spent the next two months with my time divided almost equally between ambulance flying (I did 24) and helping out with the flying in Orkney as they had a pilot shortage there at the time. With the great expansion of aviation in the north due to the oil boom we were suffering a continual turnover in pilots. The company was constantly recruiting new ones of limited experience and soon after we had trained them and they were becoming of real value to our operations they would be lured away by the many operators who were flying out of Aberdeen and were offering inflated salaries in order to get staff. Loganair's salary scale was realistic when applied to our operations but not attractive in the short-term when viewed against what others were prepared to pay in order to secure staff. It is interesting to look back and to see that all those many companies have gone into liquidation whilst Loganair goes from strength to strength!

I always enjoyed a spell in Orkney. The flying was different as most of the islands are very low which made operating in poor visibility easier, but set against that the strips are all grass and in wet weather get very muddy and are also grazed by cattle so that it was very necessary to wash the aeroplane daily, twice daily in bad conditions. About this time Loganair adopted a new colour scheme for its aircraft of white, red and black. The black band was along the lower part of the fuselage and the belly and led to someone commenting that it was to hide the cow sharn which was a definite trademark of the Orkney operation.

Like the Shetlanders, the Orcadians are a very sociable lot and I made many friends there over the years so that night stops in Kirkwall were never dull. The official attitude was very different though, perhaps because Orkney had had an inter-island service before the war and so the idea was well established in official minds. Initially, when Loganair had restarted the service after a very long lapse, caused by World War Two and then by the lack of interest by the nationalised airline in small operations, the service was run under the umbrella of the Orkney Island Shipping Company and photos of the aircraft show that the company funnel mark was carried on the tail fin. This meant that the service was subsidised by the Scottish Offfice through the shipping grant and the Orkney Islands Council only had to provide the airstrips which they very readily did. About this time Loganair became responsible for the whole operation and the shipping company dropped out of the picture. This meant that a very firm basis for the service existed in Orkney, unlike Shetland, where we felt as though the axe was ever poised above our heads.

In April a new figure appeared on the scene in Loganair in the person of Scott Grier, who joined as financial director. He brought a cold blast of realism to the organisation which, if we are really honest, was at that time run by a bunch of idealists who had a very strong belief and dedication to provide services to the Highlands and Islands but were perhaps not as concerned with the financial aspects as was necessary in a world where aviation was becoming increasingly expensive, largely due to the ever-rising costs put upon it by the bureaucrats who seemed to be more concerned with making operations more difficult than with helping what was, and still is, a very fragile but very vital service to the remoter parts of Scotland. I must admit that our first reaction to Scott was not favourable as he called into question many of our cherished ideas and none of us would have believed that he was the right person at the right time to drag the growing child that was Loganair, often screaming and protesting, into adulthood and to become what he is today, the managing director of a much changed company which now operates as British Airways Express, and not just a small outfit still out in the sticks if not having disappeared altogether as so many of our competitiors at that time have done.

At about the same time the Shetland Islands Council's chief executive, who had done so much to ensure that Shetland did not sink under the weight of the large oil companies, also left the scene and joined the British National Oil Company. The arrival of a realistic personality on the Loganair scene, and the departure of a strong one from the SIC to be replaced by a man who had not been involved in the previous acrimony, was to open the way for agreement between the two sides which was to put the whole Shetland operation on a much more secure footing for many years to come. This is not to say that all was sweet and harmonious ever after but future negotiations were to be much more realistic than had been the case in the past.

By now the very much expanded Fair Isle strip had received its airport licence and in July we started the first scheduled services to the island, running initially on Mondays and Fridays with the Saturday Bird Observatory charter, which had run regularly in the summer, also becoming a scheduled service thereby regularising a slightly grey area as tickets had been available on the charter flight since its inception. The start of a scheduled service also meant that the children from the island could get home from school in Lerwick for a week-end if they wished instead of having to remain away for the whole term as they had in the past, though the previous year the SIC had organised a half-term charter each term for them. This undoubtedly helped keep some young couples in the island who might otherwise have considered moving from the island to mainland Shetland when their children reached school age.

In July I made the first landing at the now nearly complete new Tingwall airstrip and, with difficulty, persuaded the council authorities that we should be allowed to use it for emergency ambulance flights which they were reluctant to do for legal reasons. However, after completing a suitable document indemnifying them from everything under the sun, it was agreed and I used it for the first time on 28th July to land a maternity case from Unst, and the patient gave birth within minutes of reaching the hospital. Had I to land at Sumburgh the baby would have arrived in the world either at the airport or during the road journey up to Lerwick! During the first six days of August I was to land there four more times, all with urgent cases, three of them from Whalsay and one from Unst

On the 20th I received a call from Maggie Prytherch, the Foula nurse, to say that a lady had fallen and had a very severe fracture of her arm with the end of the bone sticking out through the skin and in need of immediate evacuation. So began the longest flight for a short journey that I ever made.

Normally such a trip would have lasted about 30 minutes in all but this day Sumburgh was enveloped in fog, Foula had large fog patches all around but Tingwall, as was so often the case, was in bright sunshine as the heat of the sun in the narrow valley kept the temperature high enough to keep the fog at bay. The only safe diversion was in Norway so filling up to the limit with fuel I took off for Foula, climbing up into the clear on take-off and levelling off above the fog at about 500 feet. The top of Foula was clearly visible above the surrounding fog banks and 10 minutes after setting course I arrived at the island. The southern end was completely obscured while the north end was in sunshine, the fog stopped at the foot of the hill and the church, which is only some 400 yards from the strip, was clearly visible. As I circled I could see the nurse's van driving up to the strip gradually disappear into the mist; of the strip itself I could see nothing. The wind was light from the south and this was causing the fog to form as it moved up the slope of the island to where the strip is situated. I advised air traffic at Sumburgh that I would continue to circle Foula, hoping for a clearance, until I was down to my minimum fuel necessary to divert to Norway. In the meantime I requested a continual check on conditions at Tingwall to be passed to me.

After about an hour I noticed that there was a thinning of the fog and that I could see the road leading to the strip but not the strip itself and that the top of the fog was now only about 200 feet, which meant that the strip itself was just covered. Lining up carefully with the road I started a slow approach trying to estimate just how far to the left of the road the strip actually was. I reached the fog bank, couldn't see the strip, so climbed away to try again. The north end of the strip on Foula is the highest point on the approach and the overshoot is over the sea so I decided that I could safely descend almost to ground level and hold it for a moment or two before having to overshoot and as the edge of the fog was

Chatting after the official opening of Tingwall are Captain Whitfield (centre) and councillors, officials and guests.   Photo: © Dennis Coutts

66

clearly only yards from the strip I might just manage to see it in time to land. The next approach was made in this way and as I started to overshoot I saw the end of the strip on my left so that I passed right over the parked van and the people awaiting my arrival. I could not communicate with them as there was no radio in Foula but telepathy must have played its part as on the next attempt, made slightly more to the left, I saw the headlights of the van, which had been turned on, just in time to spot the strip, line up and land with very little visibility down the runway. The patient was loaded on board and 2 hours and 29 minutes after leaving Sumburgh I landed in Tingwall where I had to leave the aeroplane till next day before I could fly back to Sumburgh.

Ian Ray was by now well settled into Shetland flying and for the next couple of months did most of the regular flights leaving me free to concentrate on the ever-expanding administration work connected with our handling services to the oil industry and to carry out non-scheduled flights and ambulances which were by now running at an average of three a week.

On 20th October the Tingwall strip received its aerodrome licence at an official opening ceremony and we were free to restart the scheduled flights almost immediately, seeing an improvement in passenger figures as the internal traffic returned to the air service. The new inter-island ferries were also now becoming established and while as a result of this the internal traffic was never to return to its original level it was to make a useful contribution to costs.

At the beginning of December I got an ambulance call to Unst just after midnight and, whilst it was no longer possible due to increasing bureaucracy to get airborne quite as fast as had been normal in the past, I was soon on my way to Unst on a dark but clear night. As I passed the end of the Tingwall valley I could see that Stanley, the crofter who was our original fireman at the old strip and was now an SIC employee at the new one, was already lighting the flares (a task that disappeared not too long after this with the installation of electric lights).

I was soon at Unst, landed, and loading the patient was soon airborne again heading for Tingwall. As I turned into the valley I could see the flashing blue light on the ambulance as it turned off the main road showing that the new system was really beginning to work. The wind was south-west so I was able to go straight in and land. Taxi-ing to the far end to the waiting ambulance I heard Sumburgh tower trying to call me but could not get through to them myself from the ground. However as soon as I had shut down the engines Stanley came up to tell me that there was another patient waiting for me at Unst and I was to go straight back again.

This I did and on arrival at Unst found the midwife and the local doctor waiting at the strip together with a lady and her husband. I was somewhat surprised when they all boarded the aircraft but didn't ask any questions and concentrated on getting airborne again. Once in radio contact with Sumburgh again I passed the normal departure message: "Ambulance Victor Romeo out of Unst for Tingwall. Five souls on board." As we passed over Fetlar I became aware of frantic activity in the back and whilst over Whalsay was able to call Sumburgh to "amend souls on board to six" as little Margo Spence had chosen to enter this world in the skies above Shetland. A few minutes later we landed at Tingwall and the proud parents and their attendants departed for the hospital.

I finally got back to Sumburgh about 0245 feeling well pleased with the ease with which the new strip had made the operation possible.

A few weeks later I was pleased to present Margo with the christening cup with which Loganair marked all airborne births.

On the 22nd of the month I flew the Christmas mail into Foula and took the Fair Isle and Foula children home from school then took a week off to celebrate an uninterrupted holiday myself.

After being presented with a christening cup from Loganair to mark her airborne birth baby Margo Spence falls asleep in her proud mum's arms.

Photo: © R. Robertson

Chapter Eight

There was always a lighter side to flying around Shetland, both incidents seen from the aeroplane and amusement caused by the absolute ignorance of the far north shown by many officials with whom I came in contact through the coming of the oil boom.

I received a call from a government department in London one morning wishing to book a flight to Foula. The person calling said that a senior official wished to visit the island for about half-an-hour to see for himself what might be involved in carrying out some proposal then before his department. Now at that time the airstrip was complete but there was as yet no road to it and on arrival it was necessary to walk over some 200 yards of boggy land to reach the then unmade up road which ran the length of the island. Also, apart from the nurse's van, only recently lifted in by helicopter, there was no car on the island. With this in mind I could not see what might be achieved in 30 minutes and, not wanting to fly over there and then find myself waiting for a long time when I could be more usefully employed, I queried the length of waiting time requested. We laughed for days over the reply. "We've looked at the map and all that is necessary is to hire a taxi and drive up to the top of the island." As politely as possible I explained that there were no cars on the island and received the following reply. "Don't be ridiculous. If there is an airport there must be taxis," at which point the caller hung up.

Foula, probably the most remote airstrip in the United Kingdom. "If there's an airport there must be taxis".

On the appointed day the senior civil servant arrived at Sumburgh on the midday BEA flight and presented himself at the desk resplendent in his city suit and shoes. I suggested that we went over to the fire section and borrow waterproofs and wellie boots as the wind was blowing and the rain passing nearly horizontally. He seemed somewhat surprised at this, obviously expecting a car to drive up to the aeroplane to meet him. When I explained the reality of the situation he paled somewhat and suggested that if we just flew around the island he would see enough to return to London and make his report. So was born another 'expert' on the Northern Isles!

Later the same year, in June, I was asked to pick up a government minister who was attending a public meeting in Orkney in connection with oil developments, and fly him up to Shetland where he was to attend a meeting with the Shetland Islands Council the next morning. His Orkney meeting ended about 10.00 pm and it was about 10.45 pm when we finally took off for Tingwall on one of those marvellous summer evenings which are only ever seen in the north. At that time of year it is light all night, the sun setting well into the north and rising again very soon after, also in the north. Indeed, if one flies high enough, it is possible to see the sun just dip to the horizon and almost immediately rise again. As was normal, the minister was accompanied by two "bright young men" of the type so often seen who believe that civilisation stops at Watford and are terribly patronising to us benighted savages in the north!

After take-off I climbed to about 3,000 feet in order to give the party the best view possible of Orkney as we passed over the islands and set course for Tingwall with the sun still well up just to the left of the nose. We hadn't been flying for many minutes when one of the young men tapped me on the shoulder and when I'd removed my headset said: "I say pilot, I thought that the Shetlands were east of Orkney yet for the last 15 minutes we have been flying west towards the sunset." He then produced one of those ridiculous maps so often seen in which Shetland appears in a box in the Moray Firth. I explained to him that the islands were in fact north-east of Orkney and as Fair Isle and also Fitful Head on the South Mainland were by then in sight pointed them out to him, also trying to explain to him that because of the northern latitude we were at the sun did indeed set to the north. Even after we had landed at Tingwall I am sure he was not convinced!

One of the regular travellers on the inter-island service was Father Riordan, the Roman Catholic priest for Shetland. He was also a noted Celtic student and authority and one day asked if it would be possible to fly over a particular part of Fetlar where his research suggested the presence of an early reli-

70

gious site. This we did and from that grew an interest in early settlement sites which are at certain times of the year very visible from the air. Over the years I found several previously unrecorded ones and was able to pinpoint them for those interested in such things. At that time Tom Henderson was the curator of the Shetland Museum and I spent many happy and useful hours with him as a result of this sideline.

One year Shetland suffered a very heavy snow storm, many roads were blocked and much of the island came to a standstill. On my way north that morning I made a note of conditions everywhere and on reaching Unst was able to telephone Radio Shetland and give them a commentary on conditions throughout the islands. From this grew a connection with the media which lasted until I left Shetland and I was able to provide many hot news stories to both radio and the press as well as photos taken from the aeroplane as I was passing on my lawful occasions.

The most startling of these was when the *Captain John*, a large tug, caught fire off Sumburgh Head whilst towing a large oil rig and it seemed as though the whole lot would end up on the rocks. I was en route from Fair Isle at the time and was able to furnish *The Press & Journal* with pictures of an incident potentially very hazardous to the coast but which was much better handled than the more recent *Braer* incident and disaster averted.

On another occasion I was heading for Unst on an ambulance flight on the day on which the boats taking part in the Round Britain Yacht Race were due to arrrive in Lerwick on one of their compulsory stops. As we approached Bressay I noticed a large trimaran under full sail storming along and turned to the nurse to point it out to her. She said, "Where?" and when I looked again it had vanished. We flew towards where I'd last seen it and realised that it had capsized. I called air traffic and asked them to advise the Coastguard in Lerwick which they did. The Coastguard lookout had also seen it go over and had called out the lifeboat. They did request however that I check for survivors, which I did, to find one man already climbing onto the upturned hull whilst the second crew member was also visible holding onto the wreck.

Another co-operation with the Coastguard was not to have such a happy result. I was telephoned one Sunday morning to be told that there had been an explosion on the trawler *Ross Kestrel* south of Sumburgh Head and asked if I could take one of the coastguards to the area to assist until the RAF could get there. The Lerwick lifeboat was already on its way to the scene, most of the trawler's crew were in a liferaft, but two were missing. As soon as Alex Webster, then the senior man in Shetland, arrived at Sumburgh we took off, reaching the scene in about 10 minutes. There were patches of fog all around the area which made searching difficult but we quickly spotted the liferaft then being picked up by another ship that had arrived on the scene. The trawler was still afloat and was eventually boarded by men from the other boat which had arrived on the scene and salvaged. We searched for about an hour for the two missing men until a Shackleton and the lifeboat arrived on the scene but the two missing men were never found. It appeared that the trawler picked up an old torpedo in the nets and after securing it on the deck the missing men had attempted to dismantle it thereby causing it to explode.

Russian ships were a common sight around Shetland in those days, often anchored around Fetlar in large numbers as several large factory ships and a rescue tug provided services for the large number of smaller Eastern Bloc trawlers then fishing in the vicinity. In common with all Russian vessels in those days I'm sure that they were also involved in other less peaceful activities.

One morning, whilst on my regular flight into Fetlar, I noticed two of the large factory ships were moored close together with something large between them. They had tarpaulins draped from ship to ship to hide it and a RAF Shackleton was circling at a discreet distance, obviously interested. I continued with my flight around the islands and returned to Sumburgh. Soon after my return I received a telephone call from the Commanding Officer of Saxa Vord to ask if it was possible on the afternoon flight to fly low enough and near enough to the two ships to see what was under the covers. This I did and on arrival at Unst was able to 'phone him and tell him that it appeared to be a submarine.

I heard no more about this, and next day it was gone, but a few days later an anonymous sort of chap came into the office and after identifying himself asked me to go for a walk outside. He then asked me if, as I was regularly flying low in the vicinity of the various Russians, I would find out the answers to other similar questions like the submarine if he called me up and asked when he needed to know. This especially applied to the Russian naval vessels which anchored three miles east of Out Skerries in those days, often in some strength. This I continued to do until I left the islands and I'm sure became equally well known to his opposite number in the Russian Navy.

I regularly did similar but more innocuous jobs for the seal research people counting grey seals on the pupping beaches, and for the RSPB counting sea birds. On one such flight we were flying very low close to the cliffs, twisting and turning in and out of all the bays, seldom being in level flight for more than a few seconds at a time. The chap who was doing the counting was so busy he didn't notice this until we paused whilst en route to the next island at which stage he looked up, found himself totally disorientated, and promptly threw up all over me and the front of the aeroplane. I found that less than amusing!

Finally, a tale of an old lady making her very first flight in an aeroplane. It was out of the old Tingwall strip and as she was so very fascinated by it all I invited her to sit in the seat next to me. She followed all my preparations with great interest, was clearly a little worried on take-off, and no sooner were we airborne, just skimming the fence at the end of the field, when she turned to me and said very firmly: "Young man, that is quite high enough!"

Chapter Nine

Just like many previous years, 1977 started with an ambulance flight and I was to carry out 12 during January. The scheduled service was running steadily again with Ian doing most of the flying but towards the end of the month I had a very slow flight to Stornoway against a head wind to pick up members of the islands council and take them to Kirkwall for a meeting, the outbound trip taking two hours and 20 minutes; luckily the wind held and the return to Kirkwall was somewhat more rapid.

February was quiet but in March disaster struck one Sunday evening. My wife Viv, who was drying the supper dishes at the time having just seen Tanis off on the bus to Lerwick, collapsed unconscious. Dr Ian Brooker came, diagnosed a brain haemorrhage and ordered an ambulance flight to Aberdeen.

I was duty pilot and immediately started things moving to get airborne. Ian Ray heard about the flight and offered to come along too. Within 20 minutes we were on our way but passing abeam Wick I experienced a sudden feeling of loss and when a couple of minutes later Ian said, "Things aren't too good back there", I knew she was dead.

When I got back to work I threw myself into every job possible, flying whenever I could and endeavouring to blot it all out by keeping continually busy. Everyone in Shetland was very supportive of my family and myself at that time and I can never thank them enough for all they did.

Viv always loved the sea and sailing and I suggested that as a memorial people should contribute towards the new Shetland lifeboat which was then being built. Enough was raised to purchase the firefighting equipment for the boat and a suitable plate was attached to it when it was installed.

My logbook for the year shows a lot of flying but only the bare legal entries and I have little memory of any particular flights. Towards the end of the year Captain Mac told me that the chief training captain's post in Glasgow would soon become vacant as Bill Henley wished to retire from it. I told him that I would be happy to leave Shetland and take it. A Shetlander, Malcolm Bray, who was leaving the RAF, was appointed to be the number two pilot in Shetland. Ian Ray was to become senior pilot and as soon as Malcolm was trained and on the line I would move to Glasgow and take up my new post.

By the middle of March all was ready for my departure and so began a series of farewell parties as I said goodbye to the islands. At each one I was presented with a memento by the population; an engraved glass goblet from Fair

Isle; a silver tankard from Foula; a silver plaque from Unst; pictures; equipment for my boat; and from the islands council a book with the following poem in the front. I don't know who wrote it as the author's name is not on it but after all my battles with the council it some how made it alright in the end.

> *On behalf o' da guid fokk o' Shetland*
> *Da cooncil wish de 'revoir'*
> *An' 'bon chance' in dy new situation*
> *Alto' du will niver be faer*
> *Awa fae de herts o' da mony*
> *On wha's behalf du laboured so hard*
> *In da mooriest, murkiest wadder*
> *Wir burdens du willingly shared*

It's fine to ken dat nu an dan a Soothmoother comes wan o' wire ane

There were various tributes in *The Shetland Times* and the one written by Ken Foster, then Loganair's operations director, I particularly valued and reproduce here.

In carrying out some of these ambulance flights at night and in poor weather conditions, Captain Whitfield has demonstrated pilot skills of the highest order. He has shown the dedication to a humanitarian task well known in lifeboatmen and without their advantage of the moral support a crew provides."

Finally, on 16th June, I received the following letter.

Dear Captain Whitfield,

The Secretary for Trade, the Rt Honourable John Nott, as asked me to inform you that on his recommendation Her Majesty the Queen has been graciously pleased to approve the grant to you of the award of the Queen's Commendation for Valuable Service in the Air.

The award is in recognition of your outstanding contribution to the provision of an essential communications service to the people of Shetland. The Secretary of State has been informed that as Senior Pilot/Manager of Loganair in Shetland you played a key position developing air travel between the islands flying in all weathers and often landing on poorly prepared airstrips which had no navigational aids. In particular you undertook numerous emergency medical flights to fly sick people to hospital on the mainland."

Captain Alan Whitfield is presented with the Queen's Commendation for Valuable Service in the Air by the Lord Lieutenant of Lanarkshire, Colonel The Rt. Hon. Lord Clydesmuir.
Photo: © Scotsman Publications, Edinburgh, 1979

I left Shetland finally as I had arrived, sailing my boat out of the Pool of Virkie and so to Scotland where I was soon settled into the head office environment responsible for the training and testing of the entire Loganair flying staff.

My final feeling of achievement for Shetland came on 2nd April, 1979 when, flying Twin Otter *Lima Alpha*, I carried out the first Edinburgh-Tingwall scheduled service, something we hadn't even considered in our wildest dreams ten years previously.

At the beginning of 1982 I finally hung up my headset, walked away from aeroplanes and returned to the land. I was no longer an "Island Pilot".

Shetland Island Service

Reservations: Sumburgh 359 Telex 75139				
Days		**Monday**	**Tuesday & Friday**	
Flight No.		**LC723**	**LC721**	**LC725**
Sumburgh	Dep.	1215	0900	1330
Lerwick	Arr.	1225	0910	1340
	Dep.	1232	0917	1347
Whalsay	Arr.	1240	0925	1355
	Dep.	1247	0932	1402
Fetlar	Arr.	1255	0940	1410
	Dep.	1302	0947	1417
Unst	Arr.	1307	0952	1422
Flight No.		**LC724**	**LC722**	**LC726**
Unst	Dep.	1314	0959	1429
Whalsay	Arr.	1326	1011	1441
	Dep.	1333	1018	1448
Lerwick	Arr.	1341	1026	1456
	Dep.	1348	1033	1503
Sumburgh	Arr.	1358	1043	1513

LOGANAIR
The Scottish Airline

Advertisement from *The Shetland Times*, January, 1977.

77

"A busy day at Sumburgh" was the caption for this photograph taken in August, 1972 ...

78

Photos: © Dennis Coutts

. . . and this view 20 years later shows the development of Sumburgh Airport.